W.H. Macy and Christine Estabrook in a scene from the Playwrights Horizons production of "Baby With The Bathwater." Setting by Loren Sherman.

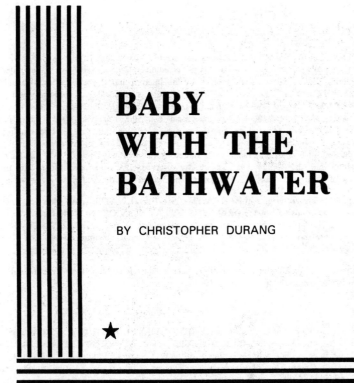

BABY
WITH THE
BATHWATER

BY CHRISTOPHER DURANG

★

DRAMATISTS
PLAY SERVICE
INC.

SPECIAL NOTE

SOUND EFFECTS

The following is a list of sound effects referenced in this play:

Children playing
Baby sounds
Baby crying
Dog barking
Dog eating
Car brakes

BABY WITH THE BATHWATER was first presented off-Broadway on November 9, 1983 by Playwrights Horizons in New York City, Andre Bishop, artistic director, Paul Daniels, managing director. The production was directed by Jerry Zaks; sets designed by Loren Sherman; costumes designed by Rita Ryack; lighting designed by Jennifer Tipton; sound designed by Jonathan Vall. Production stage manager was Esther Cohen; stage manager was Diane Ward. The cast was as follows:

HELEN .... Christine Estabrook
JOHN .... W.H. Macy
NANNY/WOMAN IN THE PARK/
    PRINCIPAL .... Dana Ivey
CYNTHIA/WOMAN IN THE PARK/
    MISS PRINGLE and SUSAN .... Leslie Geraci
YOUNG MAN........................... Keith Reddin

In the subsequent run of the play, the role of Nanny/Woman in the Park/Principal was taken over by Kate McGregor-Stewart, then by Mary Louise Wilson, then by Cynthia Darlow. The understudies were Melodie Somers and William Kux. During the play's final week Ms. Somers played the part of Helen.

BABY WITH THE BATHWATER had its world premiere at the American Repertory Theatre in Cambridge, Massachusetts on March 31, 1983, Robert Brustein, artistic director, Rob Orchard, managing director. The production was directed by Mark Linn-Baker; sets designed by Don Soule; costumes designed by Liz Perlman; lighting designed by Thom Palm; sound designed by Randolph Head. Production stage manager was John Grant-Phillips. The cast was as follows:

HELEN .... Cherry Jones
JOHN.................................. Tony Shalhoub
NANNY/WOMAN IN THE PARK/
    PRINCIPAL .... Marianne Owen
CYNTHIA/WOMAN IN THE PARK/
    MISS PRINGLE and SUSAN .... Karen MacDonald
YOUNG MAN .... Stephen Rowe

CHARACTERS

HELEN, the mother
JOHN, the father
NANNY, the nanny
CYNTHIA
A WOMAN IN THE PARK
ANOTHER WOMAN IN THE PARK
MRS. WILLOUGHBY, the principal
MISS PRINGLE, a teacher
YOUNG MAN
SUSAN

The parts of NANNY, WOMAN IN THE PARK, and MRS. WILLOUGHBY may be played by the same actress. The parts of CYNTHIA, ANOTHER WOMAN IN THE PARK, MISS PRINGLE, and SUSAN may be played by the same actress.

BABY WITH THE BATHWATER

ACT I

SCENE 1

The home of John and Helen, a couple in their late 20s or early 30s. They are standing over a bassinet.

HELEN. Hello, baby. Hello.

JOHN. It looks just like me.

HELEN. Yes it does. Smaller.

JOHN. Well, yes.

HELEN. And it looks just like me. It has my hair.

JOHN. Yes it does.

HELEN. (*Slightly worried.*) I wonder if it would have been better off having your hair?

JOHN. (*Reassuringly.*) Your hair is lovely.

HELEN. (*Touched.*) Thank you.

JOHN. You're welcome. (*They smile at one another warmly.*)

JOHN. (*Back to the bassinet.*) Hello, baby. Hello. Cooooo.

HELEN. Cooooooo. Cummmmm-quat. Cummmmm-quat!

JOHN. Hee haw. Hee haw. Daddy's little baked potato.

HELEN. Don't call the child a baked potato.

JOHN. It's a term of affection.

HELEN. It isn't. It's a *food.* No one wants to be called a baked potato.

JOHN. Well it doesn't speak English.

HELEN. The various books say that you should presume your child *can* understand you. We don't want it to have problems in kindergarten or marriage because you called it a baked potato.

JOHN. It seems to me you're losing your sense of humor.

HELEN. (*Firmly.*) I just don't want to make the child insane — that's all. Bringing up a child is a delicate thing.

JOHN. Alright, you're not a baked potato, sweet pea. (*She looks*

5

at him in horror; he senses her look.) And you're not a sweet pea either. You're a baby. Bay-bee. Bay-bee.

HELEN. I want a divorce.

JOHN. What?

HELEN. You heard me. I want a divorce.

JOHN. Are you crazy? You've read the statistics on children from broken homes. Do you want to do that to our child?

HELEN. I don't feel ready for marriage, I didn't when we got married, I should have said no.

JOHN. But we love each other.

HELEN. You have blond hair. I don't like men with blond hair. I like men with dark hair, but I'm afraid of them. I'm not afraid of you. I hate you.

JOHN. What? Is this post-partem depression?

HELEN. Don't talk about post-partem depression, you know nothing about it. (*To baby.*) Men just don't understand things, do they, sweetie pie?

JOHN. If I can't call it a potato, you can't call it a pie.

HELEN. I didn't call it a pie.

JOHN. You did. You said sweetie pie.

HELEN. Sweetie pie is an expression, it isn't a pie. You don't go into a restaurant and order sweetie pie.

JOHN. Why do you insist on winning every argument?

HELEN. If I'm right, I'm right. It has nothing to do with winning. (*To baby.*) Men don't know how to argue. That's why they always end up hitting people.

JOHN. I don't hit people.

HELEN. Boys and men hit one another constantly. They attack one another on the street, they play football, they wrestle on television, they rape one another in prison, they rape women and children in back alleys. (*To baby.*) Beware of men, darling. Be glad you're not ever going to be a man.

JOHN. That's an awful thing to say. And is it a girl? I thought it was a boy.

HELEN. We don't know what sex it is. It's too young. The doctor said we could decide later.

JOHN. You don't decide later. Gender is a fact, it's not a decision.

HELEN. That's not what the doctor said to me. He said something about the DNA molecule. They're splitting it differently now. He said if the DNA combined one way, the child would have testosterone and then we could either have it circumsized or not, depending. Or else the DNA combines with estrogen, in which case it would be a girl. Or in some cases, the DNA combines with cobalt molecules, and then the child would be radioactive for 5000 years and we'd have to send it out into orbit.

JOHN. What are you talking about?

HELEN. Can't you speak English? I'm married to an idiot. (*To baby*.) Your father is an idiot. Oh God, please let me meet a dark haired man who's smarter than I am. (*To John*.) Oh why don't you go away? I don't like you.

JOHN. I don't understand. We were very happy yesterday.

HELEN. What are you talking about? Happy? Who was happy?

JOHN. We were. We were making plans. The child's schooling, what playground to take it to, whether to let it play with toy guns, how to toilet train it.

HELEN. Oh God, toilet training. I can't face it. We'll have to hire someone.

JOHN. We don't have money to hire anyone.

HELEN. Well, we'll have to earn the money.

JOHN. But we can't earn money. I was let go from work.

HELEN. Well, you can find another job.

JOHN. I need rest, I really don't feel able to work right now.

HELEN. John, that's not practical.

JOHN. I want to go back to bed.

HELEN. But, John, you wanted to be responsible, don't you remember? Right after that week you stayed behind the refrigerator, you came to me and said, "The immaturities of my youth are over now, Helen. Let's make a baby." And then we did. Don't you remember?

JOHN. I need professional help. I want to go to McLains in Massachusetts. That's the institution James Taylor was in for a time. He seems so tranquil and calm when he gives his concerts. And he has a summer house on Martha's Vineyard. Maybe, when the doctor says I'm well enough, I could go to Mar . . .

HELEN. JOHN, LIVE UP TO YOUR RESPONSIBILITIES! (*Baby cries*.) Oh, God, it's crying. What should we do?

JOHN. Sing to it.

HELEN. (*Sings to baby sweetly, softly*.) There's no business like show business, like no business . . .

JOHN. A lullaby, sweetheart.

HELEN. I don't know any lullabys.

JOHN. (*Sings.*)

Hush little baby, don't you cry,

Mama's gonna give you a big black eye . . .

HELEN. Good heavens, those aren't the lyrics.

JOHN. I know they're not. I can't remember the right ones.

HELEN. Oh God. You're going to teach baby all the wrong lyrics to everything. It's going to have trouble with its peer group.

JOHN. Maybe we should hold it to stop it crying.

HELEN. We might drop it. I had a cocktail for breakfast. I'm not steady.

JOHN. Why did you have a cocktail?

HELEN. You're always picking on me! I'm sorry I married you. I'm sorry I gave birth to baby. I wish I were back at the Spence School.

JOHN. We love the baby.

HELEN. How can we love the baby? It won't stop that noise. (*To baby.*) Shut up, baby. Shut up. Oh God, please help us. Please make the baby stop. (*Enter Nanny, dressed in tweeds, wearing a ladylike hat and carrying a large cloth handbag.*)

NANNY. Hello. I'm Nanny.

HELEN. Oh thank goodness you've come. Please make it stop crying.

NANNY. (*Goes over to crib; in a high, soothing if odd voice.*) Helloooooooo, baby. Helllloooooo. Yeeeeeeeees. Yeeeeeees. It's Nanny. Yessssssssssssss. (*Baby stops making noise.*) That's right. That's right. I've brought you a present. (*Takes out a jar; opens it — it's a trick jar — and a large snake pops out. Baby screams in terror. John and Helen are fairly startled also. Nanny laughs.*) Ha haha haha! That surprised you, didn't it?

JOHN. See here, who are you?

HELEN. Oh my God, it's crying again. *Please* make it stop crying.

NANNY. What? I can't hear you. Child's making so much racket.

HELEN. Please. Make it stop that awful noise.

NANNY. (*High voice again.*) Quiet, little baby. Be quiet. (*No ef-*

8

fect; then she yells stridently.) SHUT UP! (*Baby is abruptly quiet; Nanny is pleased.*)

JOHN. (*Looking at the baby.*) I think you've given it a heart attack.

NANNY. No, no, it's just resting.

HELEN. Oh thank goodness it stopped.

JOHN. Who are you?

NANNY. I am the ghost of Christmas Past. Hahahahaha. No just making a joke. I get a list of all the new parents from the hospital, and then I just *descend* upon them. Now, I need Wednesday evenings off, and I'm allergic to asparagus and lobster . . .

HELEN. We never have lobster.

NANNY. And I like chunky peanut butter better than the smooth kind, but if you already have the smooth kind, we'll finish that off before you buy a new jar.

JOHN. I can't afford you.

NANNY. And I don't do windows, and I don't do floors, and I don't do laundry, but I make salmon salad and tuna salad and salad niçoise and chef salad and chunky peanut butter sandwiches, and I make my own yogurt in a great big vat.

JOHN. You can't stay here.

HELEN. But I need help. I can't cope by myself. Please, John.

JOHN. But I'm on unemployment.

NANNY. Well, we'll just get you another job.

JOHN. But what can I do?

NANNY. Why don't you become an astronaut? That pays very well. Or a football player. Or a newscaster. (*To baby.*) Wouldn't you like to see your Daddy on television, baby? Baby? (*Looks into the silent bassinet.*) I think the snake scared it. (*To baby.*) WAKE UP! (*Baby cries.*) There, that's better. (*Smiles, pleased.*)

HELEN. Please don't shout at it. It's not good for it.

JOHN. Maybe I should hold it to comfort it.

HELEN. That would be very responsible, John. That's a good boy. Good boy.

JOHN. Thank you. (*Holds baby, which stops crying.*)

HELEN. John's been fired from his job, you see.

NANNY. Well, that won't put food on the table.

HELEN. I could get a job, I suppose. But what would I do?

NANNY. Well, why don't you write a novel? "The World According to Garp" sold very well recently. Why don't you write something like that?

HELEN. Oh, that's a good idea. But I need a pencil and paper.

NANNY. Oh. Well, here's a dollar. Now you go to the store and buy some paper and a nice felt tip pen.

HELEN. Now?

NANNY. No time like the present. Right, baby?

HELEN. Oh, John, please put the baby down. I'm afraid one of us might drop it. (*To Nanny.*) I had a cocktail for breakfast, and John took some Nyquil and quaaludes.

JOHN. I get tense.

NANNY. Put the baby down, John. You're spoiling it. (*Takes it from him, puts it in bassinet.*) Now, what should we call it, do you think?

HELEN. Well, John's father's name was John, and his mother's name was Joan, and my father's name was John, and my mother's name was Hillary, and my doctor's name is Dr. Arthur Hammerstein, but I really want a woman doctor who can understand me, but it's so hard to find a doctor.

NANNY. Yes, but what about a name, a name?

HELEN. Don't you get cross with me.

NANNY. All right, we won't call the baby anything.

JOHN. We could call it John after me if it's a boy, and Helen after you if it's a girl.

HELEN. No, I don't want to call it anything now. I'm going back to bed.

NANNY. I thought you were going to buy paper and pencil to start your novel.

HELEN. I don't want to. I want to sleep.

NANNY. I gave you a dollar.

HELEN. I don't care.

NANNY. Here's another dollar. Go buy yourself an ice cream soda on the way home.

HELEN. Oh, thank you nanny. I love you. (*Hugs her, runs off.*)

NANNY. We're all going to have to be very kind to her. (*To baby.*) Don't depend on mommy, baby. She's not all there. (*To John.*) So — what can I do for you?

JOHN. I really haven't hired you yet, you know.

NANNY. You want a quick one?

JOHN. Pardon?

NANNY. Us older girls have a few tricks up our sleeves, you know. I bet I know some things your wife doesn't know.

JOHN. I don't know. I had a quaalude this morning, I don't really feel up to anything.

NANNY. It's very rude to turn me down. You might hurt my feelings.

JOHN. Well, what about the baby?

NANNY. The baby doesn't have to know anything about it. Now we haven't much time, she's getting the paper and pen and the ice cream soda.

JOHN. Well, all right, but let's not do it here. I feel uncomfortable in front of the baby.

NANNY. We could distract it. We could play loud music.

JOHN. But we might hurt its eardrums. I want to be a good father.

NANNY. Well, of course you do. I have tiny little earplugs we could put in its ears.

JOHN. Well, then, what's the point of the loud music?

NANNY. (*Thinks, but can't unravel the mystery.*) I don't know.

JOHN. This is all getting too complicated.

NANNY. (*Cheerfully.*) Very well! Let's just do it in the kitchen. Come on. (*She energetically drags John off into the kitchen. After a moment, the baby starts to cry. A young woman, rather sweet-looking but dressed shabbily, enters the apartment. Her name is Cynthia. She appears to have wandered into the apartment for no apparent reason. She is very pregnant. She walks over to the bassinet and sings sweetly to the baby to comfort it. After a few lines of the song, the baby does stop crying. Cynthia keeps singing to it for a while; her voice is pleasant and soothing.*)

CYNTHIA. (*Sings.*)
Hush, little baby,
Don't say a word,
Momma's gonna buy you a mockingbird,
And if that mockingbird don't sing,
Momma's gonna buy you a golden ring,
And if that golden ring turns brass,
Momma's gonna buy you a looking glass,
And if that looking glass gets broke,
Momma's gonna buy you a billy goat.
(*Hums. Cynthia smiles that the baby has been comforted and, still humming, wanders back out of the apartment. Lights dim.*)

11

Later that night. Dark. Baby cries. Voices of "Oh God." The lights come up. The couch has been opened up to make a bed. In the bed are Helen, Nanny, and John in nightgowns and pajamas. Nanny is sound asleep.

HELEN. Baby, we're sleeping. Now go back to sleep. John, you talk to it.

JOHN. Enough of this noise, little child. Daddy and Mommy are sleeping.

HELEN. Oh God it won't stop. Nanny, wake up. Nanny!

JOHN. Nanny! (*They poke her.*)

NANNY. (*Coming out of a dream.*) Where am I? Help! Water to the right of me, water to the left of me. Ode to a Grecian urn. (*Lies back down.*)

HELEN. Nanny, baby's calling you.

NANNY. I'm sleepy.

HELEN. Nanny, you're the nanny.

NANNY. (*Pointing to John.*) What about Tiger here?

JOHN. Don't call me Tiger.

NANNY. Tiger. Ruff. Ruff. (*Gets up.*) All right, baby. Nanny's coming. (*Picks up baby.*) Hellooooooo, baby. Helllloooooo, baby. That's right. Wheeeeeeeeeeeee. Wooooooooooooooo. Waaaaaaaaaaa. (*Keeps making these odd, if soothing, sounds softly through next dialogue. Baby does stop crying.*)

HELEN. Why did she call you Tiger?

JOHN. I don't know. She was probably dreaming.

HELEN. Oh, baby's stopped. Thank goodness for Nanny. And her Salad Niçoise was so good for dinner.

JOHN. Yes it was. Helen, I don't think this is going to work out.

HELEN. What isn't?

JOHN. Nanny.

HELEN. I think it's working out fine.

JOHN. I can't sleep three in a bed.

HELEN. John, when we're rich we'll buy a big house with an extra room for Nanny. Until then, this is fine.

JOHN. Helen, I don't think Nanny is a good person.

NANNY. I heard that.

12

JOHN. Nanny, please, we're trying to have a private conversation.

NANNY. Don't you talk behind my back. I'll hire a lawyer. We'll slap an injunction against you.

JOHN. Please, you deal with baby, and let Helen and me figure this out.

NANNY. I've finished comforting baby. (*Brusquely.*) Go to sleep, baby. (*Tosses it back into the bassinet.*) Now you say to my face that I'm not a good person.

JOHN. Well maybe that's too strong. But I think you're too rough with baby. I mean, you just threw it into the bassinet.

NANNY. Do you hear it crying?

JOHN. No, but maybe it's fainted or something.

NANNY. It's just resting.

JOHN. You keep saying that, but I think you have it fainting. And it has this look of panic on its face.

NANNY. Look, don't tell me how to handle children. I got it down.

HELEN. Nanny knows best, John. And she's helping me with my novel. She liked the first chapter, John.

NANNY. I did. I thought it showed real promise.

HELEN. And then when I sell my novel, if we get a good deal for the paperback rights, then we can buy a house in the country and maybe we can have another baby.

JOHN. Helen, Nanny seduced me this afternoon when you were out buying paper.

NANNY. That's a lie.

JOHN. It's the truth. I was unfaithful to you, Helen. (*Helen looks hurt in earnest.*) I'm sorry.

HELEN. I don't know how to cope with this.

JOHN. So you can see why I don't feel comfortable all three of us in the bed.

HELEN. (*Near tears.*) I don't know how to cope.

JOHN. I'm really sorry. It was Nanny's fault.

NANNY. He raped me!

JOHN. I didn't. That's a lie, Helen.

HELEN. I don't want to talk about this anymore! I'm going to work on my novel in the kitchen, and I'm going to pretend that I live alone. (*Exits.*)

JOHN. Well, things are in a fine mess.

13

NANNY. You told her, I didn't.

JOHN. What we did was wrong.

NANNY. Oh for God's sake, it didn't mean anything. It would've been fine if you hadn't told her.

JOHN. I felt guilty. It's wrong to cheat on your wife.

NANNY. You're such a dullard. There is no right or wrong, there's only *fun!*

JOHN. That can't be true. I mean, there are certain things that are intrinsically wrong, and when we figure out what these things are, then we are said to have values.

NANNY. Haven't you read "The Brothers Karamazov"? Ivan Karamazov realizes that because there is no God, everything is permitted.

JOHN. I don't understand.

NANNY. Everything is permitted. (*Hits the back of his head hard.*)

JOHN. Why did you do that?

NANNY. I *felt* like it. Everything is permitted. (*Laughs. Re-enter Helen, in raincoat and rainhat, holding a sheaf of papers.*)

HELEN. I'm taking my coat and the first chapter of my novel and the baby, and I'm leaving you.

JOHN. Helen, I'm sorry, it won't happen again.

HELEN. You obviously prefer Nanny to me, and so as far as I'm concerned, you can just go to hell.

NANNY. (*Genuinely meaning it.*) Oh I love arguments.

JOHN. Helen, we have to stay together for the baby.

HELEN. No, I'm taking the baby and the novel, and you won't get any of the paperback rights at all. Goodbye.

JOHN. The baby's asleep.

HELEN. Or fainted, as you said, Nanny bats it around so. (*Picks up baby.*) Mommy's going to save you now, sweetie pie.

JOHN. I have rights to the baby too.

HELEN. Baby will thank me later.

JOHN. But where will you go at this hour?

HELEN. (*At a loss.*) We'll go to . . . Marriott's Essex House.

JOHN. Our credit cards have been cancelled.

HELEN. All right. We'll sleep in the park, I don't care, I just have to leave here! Don't touch me!

JOHN. But it's freezing out. Baby will catch pneumonia.

HELEN. Well I can't help it. You don't *die* from pneumonia.

JOHN. But you do, you do die from pneumonia!

HELEN. Don't tell me what to do. I KNOW WHAT I'M DO-ING! (*Exits with baby.*)

JOHN. Helen!

NANNY. Let her go, she'll be back in a few minutes. I know these hysterical mothers.

JOHN. They're going to get very ill, it's very cold outside.

NANNY. It's bad to fuss too much as a parent, your child will grow up afraid. Let baby discover some things for itself. You want a quick one?

JOHN. What?

NANNY. You heard me.

JOHN. But it's wrong. Sexual infidelity is *wrong.*

NANNY. Wrong, right, I don't know where you pick up these phrases. Didn't they teach you about Darwin in public school? The fish came out of the water, covered with a viscous substance, and then bones and vertebrae were evolved, and then male and female, and then the egg and the ovum and the testicles and the semen, and then reproduction, and then dinosaurs, or maybe dinosaurs before that, and then local governments, and then the space program, and then nuclear power plants and now cable television and Home Box Office. *Where* do you find right and wrong in all that??? Tell me. (*Re-enter Helen, wet, with baby, wet.*)

HELEN. I fell in a puddle. I'm all wet.

NANNY. Well, if it isn't Nora five minutes after the end of "A Doll's House."

HELEN. I thought you were going to help me, and now all you do is pick on me.

JOHN. Good God, the baby's soaking wet.

HELEN. Of course, it's wet. I told you I fell in a puddle.

NANNY. Helen is the worst mother, isn't she, baby?

HELEN. Don't you say that. John, hit her for me.

JOHN. (*Very forceful suddenly.*) Now enough of all this arguing! We're going to get baby in some dry clothes, and Helen in some dry clothes, and then we're going to take Nyquil and quaaludes and get some sleep! And we will discuss all these problems in the morning. Is that clear?

HELEN. Yes, John.

NANNY. Yes, John.

JOHN. Very well. Now no more talking. (*John puts baby in bassinet and changes its clothes; Helen starts to take off her things, sneezing occasionally. Nanny exits, re-enters.*)

NANNY. I've got the Nyquil.

JOHN. Thank God.

NANNY. You have its feet in the armholes.

JOHN. The point is that it's dry, right?

NANNY. The point is to do things right.

HELEN. You said no more talking. I want to go to sleep.

JOHN. All right. But in the morning, we're going to kill Nanny. (*Nanny looks at John with suspicion.*)

HELEN. Let's just have our Nyquil and not argue anymore.

JOHN. Should we give baby Nyquil?

HELEN. Oh I don't know. What does it say on the label?

JOHN. I don't know. I can't read the small print. I need glasses.

HELEN. Well if you can't read, then there's no solution, is there?

NANNY. Why don't we just ask baby? Do you want some Nyquil, honey? Do you? Huh? (*Pause.*) It won't say. It's just staring back, hostilely.

HELEN. Oh why can't it be a happy baby? (*Notices.*) John, you've dressed it all wrong. It can barely move that way.

JOHN. I'm going to sleep now. I don't want to hear any more complaints! (*John, Helen, and Nanny get into bed.*)

NANNY. Good night everybody.

HELEN. Good night, Nanny. (*Kisses her.*) I love you. (*To John.*) I hate you.

JOHN. Good night, Helen. (*They lie down to sleep. After a moment Cynthia enters. She goes to the bassinet.*)

CYNTHIA. Hello, baby. Hellooooooo. (*The three in bed sit up and stare at her.*)

HELEN. Who are you?

CYNTHIA. I'm just so upset. I'm very poor, and I gave birth in the hospital to a darling little boy, or girl, and when I came home from the hospital, there's no heat in my apartment and there's no furniture, there's just my German shepherd. And, of course, I hadn't fed it in about a week, since I went into the hospital, so I went out to buy some baby food and some dog food. But there's no furniture, so I left the baby on the floor, and when I came back, the dog had eaten the baby. And now I don't know what to do.

16

NANNY. Have you told this story to the *New York Post*?

CYNTHIA. No.

NANNY. Well, I'd start out by doing that.

CYNTHIA. But I'm so tired now.

JOHN. What is the matter with you? Why did you leave your baby on the floor?

CYNTHIA. Please don't yell at me. I don't have any furniture!

NANNY. There, there, you poor thing. We'll get you another baby. You'll adopt.

CYNTHIA. But I'm not a fit mother.

NANNY. Everyone's allowed one mistake.

HELEN. (*Suspiciously.*) Where's the dog?

CYNTHIA. I have it right outside in the hallway. Would you like to keep it? (*She goes to the door; John springs up and blocks the door.*)

JOHN. Don't you bring that dog in here!

NANNY. Now there's no reason to hold this woman's stupidity against her dog. That's unfair. (*To Cynthia.*) Of course, we want the dog. It sounds like a good watch dog.

CYNTHIA. Well actually it's always been vicious, but you see normally I feed it. It's just that when I was in the hospital, they wouldn't let me leave.

NANNY. Administrative red tape. It's really behind so much evil and suffering in the world.

HELEN. I don't know. I think she's a terrible woman.

CYNTHIA. Oh, please, I feel so guilty. Don't hate me. I really just don't know any better. I didn't listen to anything they taught me in school. Something about equal sides of an isosceles triangle. And I don't have any furniture at home. And you have lovely furniture. Do you mind if I lie down and sleep for a moment. I'm really exhausted. (*She lies down on the sofa bed and falls asleep immediately.*)

NANNY. Poor child.

HELEN. Why is she here? We don't want her here.

NANNY. Where is your charity? The poor child is going to have to live with her stupidity all the rest of her life. Maybe she'll even have to go to prison when the police hear of it all. Surely you wouldn't begrudge her one night's sleep of safety and peace?

HELEN. Well, maybe not. But can we make her go in the morning?

NANNY. We'll see. Come, John, come to bed. Tomorrow's going to be a busy day. (*Nanny, Helen, and John lie down next to the sleeping Cynthia. Lights dim.*)

SCENE 3

Sound of dog barking viciously; baby crying. Lights up on the four of them in the sofa bed.

HELEN. Someone make that noise stop.
JOHN. Be quiet, baby.
HELEN. Is baby barking?
JOHN. Oh God, that dog. (*To Cynthia.*) Hey, you, wake up. Shut up your dog somehow.
CYNTHIA. I was having such a pleasant dream.
JOHN. Make your dog be quiet.
CYNTHIA. What dog?
JOHN. Your dog is barking.
CYNTHIA. (*Pleasantly.*) Oh yes, I hear it now. It must smell baby.
HELEN. Oh dear God.
CYNTHIA. Don't be alarmed. It's just hungry. Do you have any red meat?
JOHN. Maybe there's some red meat in the refrigerator.
CYNTHIA. Well go give it some, and then it'll stop barking. (*Smiles.*) Don't let it get your hand though. (*John exits to kitchen.*)
HELEN. Where did you get the dog?
CYNTHIA. Oh, some terrible people were beating it in the park, and I felt sorry for it, so I asked them if I could have it.
HELEN. And so they gave it to you?
CYNTHIA. Yes. They beat me up for quite a while. Twenty minutes, it seemed, maybe it was shorter, it's hard to judge time that way. And then the dog and I crawled to my apartment, and we've just been together ever since. (*John returns from the kitchen with package of chopped meat, goes into the hall to the barking dog. Barking gets worse, then ferocious eating noises occur; John comes back.*)
JOHN. It took the meat.
CYNTHIA. It really *loves* meat. I'm a vegetarian myself. I tried to make the dog eat bean sprouts and broccoli once for a while, but it didn't work out.

18

JOHN. Someone should really change baby. I think it's made a mess.

HELEN. Oh, I don't want to. Let Nanny do it.

NANNY. (*Not moving.*) I'm sleeping.

CYNTHIA. Oh, I'll do it. I love babies. (*Goes to baby.*) I had the most wonderful dream last night. I dreamt that I kidnapped your baby, and that the dog, baby and myself took a bus to Florida and had a wonderful time on the beach. (*On the word "kidnapped," the three in bed sit up and look at her with varying degrees of concern.*) I'm afraid we all got seriously sunburned in the dream, but I don't know if we died from it or not because then I woke up with the dog barking. Oh, your baby's so grumpy looking. What's the matter, baby? Don't you like me?

HELEN. It's a very grouchy baby. We're not very happy with it.

CYNTHIA. I know. I have a little toy it will like. The nurses gave it to me at the hospital. (*Holds up little red toy that jingles when she shakes it.*) Hey? It's a little red thingamajig. Isn't it cute? I don't think baby likes me. Why don't you like me, baby?

NANNY. (*With great disinterest.*) Why don't you read to it then? Baby loves to be read to. (*Exits to get into her Nanny clothes.*)

CYNTHIA. Oh all right. (*Meanders about, looking for a book.*)

HELEN. John, you better get up and go look for work.

JOHN. I just want to sleep. Leave me alone. (*Hides under pillow.*)

HELEN. John, you have responsibilities. Look at me.

CYNTHIA. Here's a book. Now if I read to you, will you promise to smile at me, baby?

JOHN. Let's get a divorce. You wanted one yesterday. Let's get one now.

HELEN. It's not practical now. Baby needs a father, and I need financial support until I finish my novel.

CYNTHIA. Chapter Seven. Shortly after Mommie Dearest won her Oscar for "Mildred Pierce," she would burst into Christopher and my room at 3 in the morning screaming, "Fire drill! Fire drill!" (*John and Helen look at Cynthia for a moment, then return to their argument.*)

JOHN. Helen, this novel idea is a pipe dream. Don't you know that?

HELEN. It is not. Nanny said my first chapter was brilliant.

NANNY. (*Off-stage.*) Well, not brilliant perhaps. But quite commercial, I'd say.

CYNTHIA. Then she'd pour gasoline on the curtains and set them on fire, while we'd scream and scream. (*Makes playful scream noises.*) Aaaaggh! Aaaaggh!

JOHN. But you can't write, don't you know that?

HELEN. What do you know? I can too! (*Nanny re-enters with Helen's still soggy sheaf of papers.*)

NANNY. Read him your first chapter then, that'll show him.

CYNTHIA. I would try to untie Christopher from his bed, but Mommie wouldn't let me.

HELEN. (*Proudly.*) Chapter One. I am born. I was born in a workhouse in London in 1853. (*Cynthia returns to reading to the baby as Helen continues to read from her novel. Nanny and John do their best to give Helen their attention, but find their focus hopelessly caught between the two novel readings. Eventually John and Nanny begin to look discouraged and disoriented by how difficult it is to follow either story.*)

HELEN. My mother, whoever she may have been, had left me at the doorstep of a wealthy man named Mr. Squire of Squireford Manor. However, wicked travelling gypsies came by the Squire's doorstep and snatched me up and left me at the workhouse. My first conscious memory is of little Nell, the cobbler's daughter, being run over by a coach and four.

CYNTHIA. As the burning curtains came closer and closer to Christopher's bed, he cried aloud, "God in heaven, save me from Mommie!" Then Mommie took out a fire extinguisher and sprayed the curtains as well as Christopher and myself. And then with tears streaming down her cheeks, Mommie screamed, "Clean up your rooms! Bad Christina! Bad Christopher! Look at this dirt!

HELEN. (*Unable to stand it anymore.*) WILL YOU BE QUIET???? I am *trying* to read from my novel.

CYNTHIA. I am reading to baby.

HELEN. I don't care what you're doing. You're a guest in this house.

CYNTHIA. Baby will grow up with no love of literature if you don't read to it.

HELEN. It's my baby, and I'll raise it as I see fit.

CYNTHIA. No, it's my baby! (*Snatches it up.*) I can see that my dream was a sign I should have it!

20

HELEN. Give it back to me at once!

CYNTHIA. No, I won't! You're not fit parents. I know I'm guilty of negligence with my baby, but it was an honest mistake. And I love babies. But you three are heartless. You don't hold the baby when it cries, you dress it wrong so it can't move in its pajamas, and you're both so inconsistent as people changing from one mood to another that you'll obviously make it crazy. That's why it never smiles. I may be forgetful, but baby has a chance with me!

HELEN. Give it back to me! (*Runs toward her.*)

CYNTHIA. Don't come near me, or I'll throw it out the window!

JOHN. Good Lord, she's insane. (*Everyone stands very still. Cynthia starts to move slowly to the door.*)

CYNTHIA. Now I'm going to leave here with baby and with the dog, and we're going to go to Florida, and you're not to follow us.

NANNY. Now let the dream be a warning. Don't stay in the sun too long. Babies have light skin.

CYNTHIA. I know what I'm doing. Come on, baby, you'll be safe with me. (*Runs out door, dog barks.*) Come on, doggie, it's just me and baby. (*Sound of dog barking, baby crying.*)

HELEN. John, what should we do?

NANNY. You could have another baby.

HELEN. John, we have to go after her.

JOHN. I need amphetamines.

HELEN. John, we haven't time.

JOHN. I told you we shouldn't have let her stay here.

HELEN. You said no such thing. And that's not the point now anyway. We've got to run after her.

JOHN. We're not dressed.

HELEN. Oh you're impossible. (*She runs out.*)

JOHN. You're right. I'm coming. (*He runs out too.*)

NANNY. (*To audience, friendly.*) Well, time to move on here, I think. I've done all I can do here. So I'll just pack. (*Notices something.*) Oh, she forgot her little red toy. Oh, too bad. (*Picks toy up, reads something on it.*) "Caution. Keep away from children. Contains lead, asbestos, and red dye #2." (*Laughs.*) Well, I guess it isn't meant as a child's toy at all then. (*Looks at it with utter bafflement.*) But what would it be meant as, I wonder? (*Energized by an idea:*) Maybe it *is* a toy, and the cautionary warning is *satiric!*

21

(*Tosses the toy into bassinet.*) Hard to tell. So many mysteries. But children can survive it all, they are sturdy creatures. They ebb and flow, children do; they have great resiliency. (*Warmly.*) They abide and they endure. (*Re-enter John and Helen, holding baby. They are giddy with relief.*)

JOHN. We got it.

NANNY. Oh, did you?

HELEN. Yes, the stupid girl ran right in front of a bus, it ran right over her.

JOHN. Squashed her.

HELEN. Baby was just lucky and fell between the wheels.

NANNY. Oh that was lucky. Children are sturdy creatures, they ebb and flow.

HELEN. The dog was still living, so John pushed it in front of an oncoming car, and now it's dead too.

JOHN. The motorist was *real* angry. But it seemed too complicated to explain, so we just grabbed baby and ran.

HELEN. Thank goodness. (*Looks at baby.*) Baby looks so startled. It's been a busy day, hasn't it? Yessss.

JOHN. Nanny, Helen and I were talking while we ran back here, and things are going to be different now. The immaturities of my youth are over and I'm going to take the responsibility of being a father, and Helen is going to be a mother. And we're not letting anymore crackpots into our home.

HELEN. That's right, John.

JOHN. And so, Nanny, I'm going to have to ask you to leave now. Helen and I have both decided that you're insane.

NANNY. (*Crosses to them.*) When it cries, you hold it. You should feed it regularly. You should keep it clean. Be consistent with it. Don't coo one minute and shout the next.

HELEN. I'm giving up my career as a novelist to care for baby. And any resentment I feel I won't ever show.

NANNY. Well that all sounds excellent. Goodbye, Helen. Goodbye, Tiger.

HELEN. Goodbye, Nanny. We love you.

JOHN. Goodbye. (*Nanny smiles fondly and waves. Then exits.*)

HELEN. (*After a moment.*) Oh, John. I feel so lonely now.

JOHN. We have each other. And baby.

HELEN. That's true. I wish I didn't have a baby and that I had written "Scruples" instead.

JOHN. Well, I wish I were in McLains, but I thought we were going to be positive about things from now on.

HELEN. You're right. I was just kidding. Let's be parents now. Hellooo, baby. (*They put baby back into bassinet.*)

JOHN. (*To baby.*) Helllooo. Baby looks so startled.

HELEN. Well, of course, it's been a terrifying day. Baby had never even seen a bus before, let alone been under one. (*Lovingly, to the baby.*) Don't worry, sweetie pie. Mommy'll protect you from now on. She'll protect you from buses, and from dogs, and from crazy people; and from everything and anything that goes bump in the night.

JOHN. (*Playfully.*) Bump, bump, bump.

HELEN. (*Fondly.*) That's right, John.

JOHN. And Daddy loves you too, my little baked potato.

HELEN. (*Suddenly absolutely furious.*) I TOLD YOU NOT TO CALL IT A BAKED POTATO!!!

JOHN. I'm sorry, I'm sorry. Jesus. You mustn't raise your voice that way around baby. You'll make it deaf or something.

HELEN. I'm sorry. I feel better now.

JOHN. Okay, we'll forget it. (*To baby.*) All over, baby. You're safe now, my little bak- . . . baby. No more shouting. Everything's fine. Can you smile for daddy?

HELEN. Or mommy?

JOHN. Can you smile for mommy and daddy? Here's a nice little red toy. (*Holds up the red toy.*) Won't that make you smile? Huh? Oh why won't it smile? SMILE, damn it, SMILE!

HELEN. Smile, baby!

BOTH. (*Angry.*) SMILE! SMILE! SMILE! SMILE!

HELEN. (*Pleased.*) Oh, John, look, it's smiling.

JOHN. That's right, baby.

HELEN. Do you think it's just pretending to smile to humor us?

JOHN. I think it's too young to be that complicated.

HELEN. Yes, but why would it smile at us when we shouted at it?

JOHN. I don't know. Maybe it's insane.

HELEN. I wonder which it is. Insane, or humoring us?

JOHN. Look, it's still smiling. Maybe it likes the toy. Do you like the toy, baby? Here, you play with it a while, baby. It

23

makes a funny noise, doesn't it? Tingle tangle. Tingle tangle. (*The baby throws the toy out of the bassinet.*) Oh, it doesn't like the toy.

HELEN. What a fussy baby. (*Playfully.*) Fussy baby. Fussy baby.

JOHN. (*Happy.*) Oh, it's still smiling.

HELEN. Fussy baby.

JOHN. Fussy wussy wussy.

BOTH: (*Fondly.*) Fussy wussy wussy baby. Fussy wussy wussy baby. (*Lights dim.*)

ACT II

Scene 1

A park bench. Three women in park playground. The sounds of children playing. On the bench are: Helen, the mother from the previous scenes; she is looking straight ahead, smoking a cigarette, and seems unhappy, hostile. Next to her, and presently not paying attention to her, are Angela, a sweet, drably dressed woman (can be played by same actress who played Cynthia in first part, though try to make her plain) and Kate, a bright, sharp-tongued woman with a scarf tied around her head (she can be played by same actress who played Nanny, but try to make her look noticeably different). Angela and Kate are looking straight out, watching their children, who are placed (in their and our imaginations) out in the audience. Kate is knitting.

KATE. Be careful, Billy!

ANGELA. That's your son?

KATE. Yes. Billy. He has my eyes and mouth, and his father's nose.

ANGELA. (*Looking, squinting.*) Yes, I can see that. Of course, I've never seen your husband's nose, but he does have your mouth and eyes.

KATE. Don't hang upside down, Billy! You'll crack your head open. (*To Angela.*) He's reckless, just like his uncle Fred.

ANGELA. Oh. Is that his favorite uncle?

KATE. No. He's never met Fred. Fred is dead. Is that your little girl?

ANGELA. Yes. Susie. Watch your head, Susie! It's such a full time job looking after children.

KATE. Yes it is. Susie's a pretty child. (*Stares at Angela; suspiciously.*) Is her father very handsome?

ANGELA. Yes. His whole family is very nice looking.

KATE. Oh that's nice. Nobody in our family is particularly good looking. Except for Fred, sort of, though you'd never know it from the way he ended up, all squashed that way.

ANGELA. How did he die?

KATE. Part of the roller skating craze. He didn't know how, and he skated right under a crosstown bus. (*Calls out.*) Be care-

25

ful, Billy! (*Back to conversation.*) I don't think there's such a thing as a homely child, do you? I mean Billy may well grow up to be *quite* homely, but right now he's really very cute. And your daughter is downright pretty.

ANGELA. Thank you. (*Calls.*) Be careful of your face, Susie. Don't fall down on it.

HELEN. I have a child too, you know.

KATE. What?

HELEN. No one has asked me about my child.

KATE. Well no one was talking to you.

HELEN. Well I'm a human being. I deserve courtesy.

KATE. Where is your child?

HELEN. That's her lying on the ground. (*Calls.*) Get up, Daisy! Stop acting like a lump.

KATE. What's the matter with her?

HELEN. She's very depressed. She falls asleep all the time. You put her in the bathtub, she falls asleep. You put her on the toilet, she falls asleep. She's a depressing child. Get up, Daisy! Maybe one of the boys would poke her for me.

ANGELA. Maybe she has narcolepsy.

HELEN. You get that from a venereal disease, don't you? You're trying to say something nasty about me, aren't you?

ANGELA. Narcolepsy is a disease. Where people fall asleep. You should take your daughter to a doctor.

HELEN. All diseases are psychological. I'm not going to waste money on some dumb doctor who can't do anything about anything. She sleeps because she doesn't want to be awake. She has no "joie de vivre." GET UP, DAISY! Hey, you, boy, the one with the stick . . . can you get my daughter up?

KATE. (*Staring; after a bit.*) Billy, don't put the stick there, that's nasty.

ANGELA. Why isn't she moving?

HELEN. She's willful. GET UP YOU LUMP OF CLAY! (*To boy.*) Tug her hair a little.

KATE. Billy, leave the little girl alone and go play on the jungle gym. (*To Helen.*) I don't want you encouraging my son to pick on women. That's not a very good thing to teach.

ANGELA. She still hasn't moved. Maybe she's fainted.

HELEN. She just does this to annoy me. It's very successful. (*Calls.*) YOU'RE VERY SUCCESSFUL, DAISY. YOU'RE

26

GETTING THROUGH. (*Back to them.*) It's passive aggression. I do it with my husband. He says to me, did you make dinner, I lie down on the rug and don't move. He says, get up, I don't move a muscle. He gets on top of me and starts to screw me, I pretend it isn't happening. She gets it from me. (*Yells.*) DO AS I SAY NOT AS I DO, DAISY, I'VE TOLD YOU THAT!

KATE. That's no way to bring up a child.

HELEN. What do you know? Do you want a fat lip? Don't cross me, I could do something terrible to your child.

KATE. What did you say?

HELEN. (*Suddenly coy and girlish.*) Oh nothing. My bark's worse than my bite. (*Calls viciously.*) Get up, Daisy! (*Sings, to Daisy, rather sweetly.*)

Daisy, Daisy,

Give me your answer, do,

I'm half crazy,

All for the love of you . . .

(*Hostile, to Kate & Angela.*) Sing. (*They hesitate.*) SING!

ALL THREE. (*Kate & Angela, uncomfortable.*)

It won't be a stylish marriage,

I can't afford a carriage,

But you'll look sweet . . .   HELEN. (*Echoing.*) Sweet.

Upon the seat . . .   HELEN. Seat.

Of a bicycle built for two.

HELEN. Did she move?

ANGELA. I think her arm twitched a little.

HELEN. Oh, I bet she heard it. She loves that song. Don't you, Daisy? Well, I have to go home now. (*Sweetly.*) Goodbye. (*Calls out to Daisy.*) Get up, Daisy, we're going home, mother can't stand the park another minute. Get up! (*Getting wild.*) Get up, damn you, get up! All right, Daisy, I'll give you til five and then I'm gonna step on your back. You listening? 1. . . . 2. . . .3. . . .

ANGELA. Get up, Daisy.

HELEN. . . . 4. . . . 4½. . . . 4¾. . . . Oh, look, there she goes.

KATE. My God, she's running *fast*. (*They turn their heads in unison quickly, watching Daisy run out of sight.*)

HELEN. She's like that. Very inconsistent. One minute catatonic, the next minute she *moves* like a comet.

ANGELA. My God, she's running right toward that bus!

27

HELEN. Yes, she's always been drawn to buses. She's always running right out in front of them. Usually the driver stops in time.

KATE. My God, it's going to hit her!

HELEN. Well, it'll probably be fine. (*Kate & Angela watch horrified, then there's a shriek of brakes, and they relax, horrified but relieved.*)

KATE. Thank God.

ANGELA. It came so close.

HELEN. This happens all the time. I get quite used to it. (*Suddenly switches to real maternal feelings, gets very upset.*) Oh my God, Daisy. Oh my God, she was almost killed. Oh God. Oh God. (*Weeps.*) Daisy, I'm coming, darling, don't move, honey, mommy's coming. (*Runs off, very upset.*)

KATE. Good grief.

ANGELA. Well, at least the child's safe.

KATE. Do you think we should do something?

ANGELA. What do you mean?

KATE. I don't know. Contact social welfare or something.

ANGELA. I don't know. Maybe it's not her child. Maybe she's only babysitting.

KATE. I don't think so.

ANGELA. I don't think we should get involved.

KATE. Alright, we won't do anything about her. We'll wait until we read about the child *dead* in the newspaper.

ANGELA. I read about that child they found dismembered in the garbage cans outside the 21 Club. CBS is going to make a TV movie about it.

KATE. I don't think television should exploit the sufferings of real people like that.

ANGELA. But they've got all those hours of programming to do. They've got to fill it up with something.

KATE. I suppose.

ANGELA. I wouldn't like to be a television executive. You'd have to have ideas all the time, and then after a while if people don't like your ideas, they fire you.

KATE. This is really off the point of what we should do about that poor child.

ANGELA. I don't like to think about it.

KATE. Well, that won't help the child.

ANGELA. I don't like to concentrate on one thing for too long a period of time. It makes my brain hurt.

KATE. I don't think either the mother or the child are mentally well.

ANGELA. No, they're probably not, but who is nowadays? Everything's so outside our control. Chemical explosions in Elizabeth, New Jersey. Somebody killed Karen Silkwood. There are all these maniacs stalking Dolly Parton, the poor woman doesn't feel like *singing* anymore. John Hinkley, David Berkowitz, Ronald Reagan. It's so difficult to maintain "joie de vivre" in the face of such universal discouragement. (*Looks glum for a moment.*) I have to take a mood elevator. (*Takes a pill.*) I have this pharmacist friend, he gives me all sorts of things. I should be cheerful in a few minutes. (*Waits for pill to take effect.*)

KATE. (*Edging away.*) Well, fine. We'll do nothing then. I'll look forward to the CBS movie about the child under the bus. (*Calls.*) Come on, Billy, we're going home. *Billy!* Don't put the stick there, that's rude. Leave Susie alone. (*Shocked.*) Billy! Don't put *that* there either, that's *very* rude. Now put that back. (*To Angela.*) I'm sorry. He's just that age now.

ANGELA. Oh that's all right. He probably meant it affectionately. I always think sex and affection are somehow connected, don't you?

KATE. Well, no, not really.

ANGELA. Oh, I do. People need affection, you know. Susie, come give mommy a hug. (*Lights dim.*)

SCENE 2

Back in the home of Helen and John. The room, though, is filled with many toys, some of them broken. There is also a pile of what seems to be laundry in clear audience view. Two little legs with red sneakers are partially visible, sticking out of the laundry pile. John and Helen are talking.

JOHN. Well, I'm very upset. That's all I can say.

HELEN. I know. You've said that, you've said that. Get on with it.

JOHN. I mean, I just don't think we're good parents.

HELEN. Why do you say that? Did the bus run over the child? No. Did a bus run over her last week? No.

JOHN. Why does she keep running to buses? What's the matter with her?

HELEN. Nothing is the matter with her. She's just depressed. We have to cheer her up. (*Crosses to pile of laundry, speaks to it.*) Cheer up, Daisy! You're depressing us.

JOHN. And why does she lie in this pile of laundry all the time? Do you think that's normal?

HELEN. Daisy is just going through a phase. She thinks she's an inanimate object. She thinks she's a baked potato because of what you said to her when she was a baby. (*To pile of laundry.*) You're not a baked potato, sweet pea. You're mommy's little darling. Mommy loves you. Mommy doesn't mind that she's not a novelist or that she's stayed in a bad marriage just for your sake. She's willing to make that sacrifice. (*Stares at laundry.*) Uh, you see how unresponsive she is. It's enough to make you want to shake and bake her.

JOHN. Helen, we can't talk about the child that way. Did you hear what you just said?

HELEN. I was making a point, John. I'm not talking about actually cooking her. You have no sense of irony. (*To Daisy.*) We're not going to eat you, Daisy. Mommy was speaking figuratively.

JOHN. Speaking of shake and bake, have you made dinner yet?

HELEN. Have I made *dinner* yet? (*Very nasty, utterly furious.*) Well, now, let me see. I can't remember. You were at unemployment, and then I was at the playground, and then Daisy tried to run in front of a bus—now I remember all these events . . . but as to dinner. I'm going to have to lie down and think. (*She lies down on the floor and won't move.*)

JOHN. Helen, don't do this again. You know it makes me furious. Helen, stop staring at the ceiling. Helen! HELEN! (*Stares; has quick fit.*) GODDAM IT! (*Takes one of Daisy's toys, smashes it.*) I've smashed one of Daisy's toys, Helen, do you want me to smash another one? Helen, get up! Look at me. All right, Helen, I'm going to smash another one of her toys . . . (*Hears himself.*) Good God, listen to me. What's happened to us? Helen, we're ruining that poor child. I'm going to take her and leave

30

you. We've got to get away from you. (*Goes to pile of laundry.*)
Get up, Daisy, Daddy loves you. Daisy, get up. (*Sings sweetly.*)
Daisy, Daisy . . . GODDAM IT, GET UP! (*Starts to tie laundry
and Daisy into a manageable bundle.*) Okay, Daisy, I'll just have to
carry you. Helen, I'm taking Daisy and the laundry and we're
leaving you. (*Slings laundry over his shoulder.*) I don't know where
we're going, but we've got to get away. Helen, can you hear
me? Helen, we're leaving you. Goodbye.

HELEN. (*Sits up.*) And you'll never get any of the paperback
rights! (*Lies down again.*)

JOHN. There aren't any paperback rights, Helen! You live in a
fool's paradise. We're leaving now. (*Starts to leave.*) I don't know
where we're going, but we're going somewhere. (*Stops.*) I just
need a drink first, though. Where's the vodka, Helen? Helen?
(*Puts laundry down.*) Daisy, do you know where the vodka is?
Daisy? Helen? Daisy? Helen? GODDAM IT, I'M TALKING
TO YOU PEOPLE, ARE YOU DEAF? (*Sits on floor.*) Oh God,
how did I get in this position? Where is the vodka?

HELEN. (*Sits up.*) It's in the toy duck. (*Does speech exercise.*) Toy
duck, toy duck, toy duck. (*Lies down again.*)

JOHN. Oh right. Thank you. (*Goes to toy duck, reaches into it,
takes out bottle of vodka.*) Why can't we have a liquor cabinet like
normal people? (*Takes a big couple of swallows from the vodka.*)
Want some, Helen? (*No response.*) Daisy? Daisy? (*Bitter.*) She's
not a baked potato, she's a 20 per cent cotton, 80 per cent poly-
ester pile of . . . (*At a loss.*) pooka-poo.

HELEN. (*Sits up.*) Pooka-poo, pooka-poo. Toy duck. Toy
duck. Polly wolly windbag! Polly wolly windbag! Mee, mae,
mah, moh, moo. Mee, mae, mah, moh, moo.

JOHN. Oh, Helen, you're talking again. I'm sorry I asked you
about dinner. Want a cocktail?

HELEN. Thanks I'm too tired. (*Lies down.*)

JOHN. (*Sings.*)
Daisy, daisy, give me your answer, do . . .
(*Next song.*)
Hush, little baby, don't you cry,
Mamma's gonna give you a big black eye . . .

HELEN. (*Lying down, but calm.*) John, those aren't the lyrics.

JOHN. I know. I just don't know the lyrics. (*Sings.*)

And if that big black eye turns purple . . .
Mama's gonna give you a . . .
(*Spoken.*) What rhymes with purple?
HELEN. (*Sits up.*) I don't know. I'm not a rhyming dictionary.
Ask Daisy.
JOHN. Daisy, honey, what rhymes with purple? Daisy? Daisy,
what rhymes with purple? Daisy? (*Listens; apparently hears an an-
swer.*) She says she doesn't know.
HELEN. (*Slightly hopeful.*) Well at least she spoke today. That's
something.
JOHN. (*Cheered.*) Yes, that is something. (*Drinks. Lights fade.*)

Scene 3

*A desk and chair. The Principal is seated. She is dressed hand-
somely, but looks somewhat severe.*

PRINCIPAL. (*To intercom.*) You can send Miss Pringle in now,
Henry. (*Enter Miss Pringle, a sympathetic-looking teacher.*) I love
having a male secretary. It makes it all worth while. (*Into intercom.*) Sharpen all the pencils please, Henry. Then check the cof-
fee pot. Hello, Miss Pringle, how are you?
MISS PRINGLE. I'm fine, Mrs. Willoughby, but I wanted to
talk to you about Daisy Dingleberry.
PRINCIPAL. Oh yes, that peculiar child who's doing so well
on the track team.
MISS PRINGLE. Yes, she runs very quickly, but I felt I
should . . .
PRINCIPAL. Wait a moment, would you? (*Into intercom.*) Oh,
Henry, check if we have enough non-dairy creamer for the cof-
fee, would you? Then I want you to go out and buy my husband a birthday present for me, I don't have time. Thank you,
sweetie. (*Back to Pringle.*) Now, I'm sorry, what were you saying?
MISS PRINGLE. Well, I'm worried about Daisy. She's doing
very well in track, and some days she does well in her classes,
and then some days she just stares, and then she's absent a lot.
PRINCIPAL. Yes. Uh huh. Uh huh. Yes, I see. Uh huh. Uh
huh. Go on.

MISS PRINGLE. Well, it's her summer essay, you know . . . "What I Did Last Summer"?

PRINCIPAL. (*With great interest.*) What did you do?

MISS PRINGLE. No, no, no, it's the *topic* of the essay: what you did last summer.

PRINCIPAL. Mr. Willoughby and I went to the New Jersey sea shore. He was brought up there. It brings back fond memories of his childhood. Bouncing on his mother's knee. Being hugged, being kissed. Mmmmmm. Mmmmmm. (*Makes kissing sounds, hugs herself; into intercom.*) Henry, sweetie, I want you to buy my husband underwear. Pink. The bikini kind. Calvin Klein, or something like that. Or you could use your "Ah Men" catalog if it wouldn't take too long. Mr. Willoughby is a medium. Thank you, Henry. (*To Pringle.*) I'm sorry, what were you saying?

MISS PRINGLE. About Daisy's essay.

PRINCIPAL. What about it?

MISS PRINGLE. Well . . .

PRINCIPAL. Wait a moment, would you? (*To intercom.*) Henry, I mean Mr. Willoughby is a medium *size,* I don't mean he holds seances. (*Laughs; to Pringle.*) I didn't want there to be any misunderstanding. I don't think there was, but just in case. I myself am into black magic. (*Takes out a black candle. To intercom.*) Henry, I have taken out a black candle and I am thinking of you. (*To Pringle.*) Do you have a match?

MISS PRINGLE. No, I'm sorry. About Daisy's essay.

PRINCIPAL. I'm all ears.

MISS PRINGLE. Well . . .

PRINCIPAL. Which is a figure of speech. As you can indeed see, I am a great deal more than just ears. I have a head, a neck, a trunk, a lower body, legs and feet. (*To intercom.*) I have legs and feet, Henry. I hope you're working quickly.

MISS PRINGLE. Pay attention to me! Focus your mind on what I'm saying! I do not have all day.

PRINCIPAL. Yes, I'm sorry, I will. You're right. Oh, I *admire* strong women. I've always been afraid I might actually be a lesbian, but I've never had any opportunity to experiment with that side of myself. You're not interested, are you? You're single. Perhaps you *are* a lesbian.

MISS PRINGLE. I'm not a lesbian, thank you, anyway.

PRINCIPAL. Neither am I. I just thought maybe I was. (*Into intercom.*) Henry, you don't think I'm a lesbian, do you? (*Listens.*) The intercom only works one way, it needs to be repaired. Of course, Henry's a mute anyway.

MISS PRINGLE. Mrs. Willoughby, please, put your hand over your mouth for a moment and don't say anything.

PRINCIPAL. I'm all ears. (*Puts her hand over her mouth.*)

MISS PRINGLE. Good, thank you. I was disturbed by Daisy's essay. I want you to listen to it. "What I Did For My Summer Vacation." By Daisy Dingleberry. "Dark, dank rags. Wet, fetid towels. A large German shepherd, its innards splashed across the windshield of a car. Is this a memory? Is it a dream? I am trapped, I am trapped, how to escape. I try to kill myself, but the buses always stop. Old people and children get discounts on buses, but still no one will ever kill me. How did I even learn to speak, it's amazing. I am a baked potato. I am a summer squash. I am a vegetable. I am an inanimate object who from time to time can run very quickly, but I am not really alive. Help, help, help. I am drowning, I am drowning, my lungs fill with the summer ocean, but still I do not die, this awful life goes on and on, can no one rescue me." (*Miss Pringle and Principal stare at one another.*) What do you think I should do?

PRINCIPAL. I'd give her an A. I think it's very good. The style is good, it rambles a bit, but it's unexpected. It's sort of an intriguing combination of Donald Barthelme and Sesame Street. All that "I am a baked potato" stuff. I liked it.

MISS PRINGLE. Yes, but don't you think the child needs help?

PRINCIPAL. Well, a good editor would give her some pointers, granted, but I think she's a long way from publishing yet. I feel she should stay in school, keep working on her essays, the school track team needs her, there's no one who runs as fast. I think this is all premature, Miss Pringle.

MISS PRINGLE. I feel she should see the school psychologist.

PRINCIPAL. I am the school psychologist.

MISS PRINGLE. What happened to Mr. Byers?

PRINCIPAL. I fired him. I thought a woman would be better suited for the job.

MISS PRINGLE. But do you have a degree in psychology?

PRINCIPAL. I imagine I do. I can have Henry check if you insist. Are you sure you're not a lesbian? I think you're too forceful, it's unfeminine. And I think you're picking on this poor child. She shows signs of promising creativity, and first you try to force her into premature publishing, and now you want to send her to some awful headshrinker who'll rob her of all her creativity in the name of some awful God of normalcy. Well, Miss Pringle, here's what I have to say to you: I will not let you rob Daisy Dingleberry of her creativity, she will not see a psychologist as long as she is in this school, and you are hereby fired from your position as teacher in this school. Good day! (*To intercom.*) Henry, come remove Miss Pringle bodily from my office, sweetie, would you?

MISS PRINGLE. No need to do that. I can see myself out. Let me just say that I think you are insane, and I am sorry you are in a position of power.

PRINCIPAL. Yes, but I *am* in a position of power! (*To intercom.*) Aren't I, Henry? Now get out of here before I start to become violent.

MISS PRINGLE. I am sorry you will not let me help this child.

PRINCIPAL. Help this child! She may be the next Virginia Woolf, the next Sylvia Plath.

MISS PRINGLE. Dead, you mean.

PRINCIPAL. (*Screams.*) Who cares if she's dead as long as she publishes? Now, get out of here! (*Blackout.*)

SCENE 4

A blank stage, a simple white spot. From a loudspeaker at the back of the auditorium we hear a male voice — serious, sympathetic in a detached, business-like manner.

VOICE. Come in please. (*Enter a young man in a simple, modest dress. His haircut, shoes and socks, though, are traditionally masculine. He looks out to the back of the auditorium to where the voice is originating from. The young man seems shy, polite, tentative.*) State your name please.

YOUNG MAN. Daisy.

VOICE. How old are you?

DAISY. I'm seventeen.

VOICE. I wish I had gotten your case earlier. Why are you wearing a dress?

DAISY. Oh, I'm sorry, am I? (*Looks, is embarrassed.*) I didn't realize. I know I'm a boy . . . young man. It's just I was so used to wearing dresses for so long that some mornings I wake up and I just forget. (*Thoughtfully, somewhat to himself.*) I should really just clear all the dresses out of my closet.

VOICE. Why did you used to wear dresses?

DAISY. Well that's how my parents dressed me. They said they didn't know what sex I was, but it had to be one of two, so they made a guess, and they just guessed wrong.

VOICE. Are your genitals in any way misleading?

DAISY. No, I don't believe so. I don't think my parents ever really looked. They didn't want to intrude. It was a kind of politeness on their part. My mother is sort of delicate, and my father rests a lot.

VOICE. Did you think they acted out of politeness?

DAISY. Well, probably. It all got straightened out eventually. When I was eleven, I came across this medical book that had pictures in it, and I realized I looked more like a boy than a girl, but my mother had always wanted a girl or a best seller, and I didn't want to disappoint her. But then somedays, I don't know what gets into me, I would just feel like striking out at them. So I'd wait til she was having one of her crying fits, and I took the book to her — I was twelve now — and I said, "Have you ever seen this book? Are you totally insane? Why have you named me Daisy? Everyone else has always said I was a boy, what's the *matter* with you?" And she kept crying and she said something about Judith Krantz and something about being out of Shake-n-Bake chicken, and then she said, "I want to die"; and then she said, *Perhaps* you're a boy, but we don't want to jump to any hasty conclusions, so why don't we just wait, and we'd see if I menstruated or not. And I asked her what that word meant, and she slapped me and washed my mouth out with soap. Then she apologized and hugged me, and said she was a bad mother. Then she washed *her* mouth out with soap. Then she tied me to the kitchen table and turned on all the gas jets, and said it would be just a little while longer for the both of us. Then my father came home and he turned off the gas jets and untied me. Then when he asked if dinner was ready, she lay on the kitchen floor and wouldn't move, and he said, I guess not, and then he sort of crouched next to the refrigerator and tried to read a book, but I don't think he was really reading, because he never turned any of the pages. And then eventually, since nothing else seemed to be happening, I just went to bed. (*Fairly long pause.*)

VOICE. How did you feel about this?

DAISY. Well I knew something was wrong with them. But then they meant well, and I felt that somewhere in all that, they actually cared for me — after all, she washed *her* mouth with soap too, and he untied me. And so I forgave them because they meant well. I tried to understand them. I felt sorry for them. I considered suicide.

VOICE. That's the end of the first session. (*Lights change. In view of the audience, Daisy removes his girl's clothing and changes into men's clothing — pants and a shirt, maybe a sweater. As he changes we hear the "Hush little baby" theme played rather quickly, as on a speeded-up music box. The change should be as fast and as simple as possible. Lights come up and focus on Daisy again.*) This is your second session. How old are you?

DAISY. I'm nineteen now.

VOICE. Why have you waited two years between your first and second sessions? And you never called to cancel them. I've been waiting here for two years.

DAISY. I'm sorry. I should have called. I was just too depressed to get here. And I'm in college now, and I've owed this paper on Jonathan Swift and "Gulliver's Travels" for one and a half *years*. I keep trying to write it, but I just have this terrible problem *beginning* it.

VOICE. In problems of this sort, it's best to begin at the beginning, follow through to the middle, and continue on until the ending.

DAISY. Ah, well, I've tried that. But I don't seem to get very far. I'm still on the first sentence. Jonathan Swift's "Gulliver's Travels" is a biting, bitter work that . . ." I keep getting stuck on the "That."

VOICE. I see you're wearing men's clothing today.

DAISY. (*With a sense of decisiveness.*) I threw all my dresses away. And I'm going to change my name from Daisy. I'm considering Francis or Hilliary or Marion.

VOICE. Any other names?

DAISY. Rocky.

VOICE. Have you seen your parents lately?

DAISY. I try not to. They call me and they cry and so on, but I hold the receiver away from my ear. And then I go next to the refrigerator and I crouch for several days.

VOICE. How are you doing in school?

DAISY. I'm not even sure I'm *registered*. It's not just the Jonathan Swift paper I owe. I owe a paper comparing a George Herbert poem with a Shakespeare sonnet; I owe a paper on characterization in "The Canterbury Tales"; and an essay on the American character as seen in Henry James' "Daisy Miller." (*Daisy looks off into the distance, and sings softly.*)

Daisy, Daisy,

Give me your answer, do,

I'm half-crazy . . .

(*He looks grave, sad, repeats the line:*)

I'm half-crazy . . .

(*His sadness increases, he speaks slowly:*)

" 'I am half-sick of shadows,' said the Lady of Shallot."

VOICE. You sound like an English major.

DAISY. (*His attention returns to the voice.*) Yes. I learned a certain love of literature from my parents. My mother is a writer. She is the author of the Cliff Notes to "Scruples" and "Princess Daisy." And my father liked reading. When he was next to the refrigerator, he would often read. I like reading. I have this eerie dream, though, sometimes that I'm a baby in my crib and somebody is reading aloud to me from what I think is "Mommie Dearest," and then this great big dog keeps snarling at me, and then this enormous truck or bus or something drops down from the sky, and it kills me. (*With a half-joking, half-serious disappointment he's not dead.*) Then I always wake up.

VOICE. That's the end of our second session. (*The lights change abruptly. From now on, these abrupt light changes—probably a center spot with side lighting that switches side to side on each change—will represent time passing and finding Daisy in the midst of other sessions. There should not be blackouts, and though Daisy should speak only once the lighting shift has completed, these changes should happen quickly.*)

DAISY. Doctor, I'm so depressed I can hardly talk on the phone. It's like I can only function two hours a day at maximum. I have this enormous desire to feel absolutely nothing.

VOICE. That's the end of our third session. (*Lights change abruptly.*)

DAISY. You know, when I *do* get up, I sleep with people obsessively. I'm always checking people out on the street to see who I can sleep with.

VOICE. Eventually you'll get a lot of venereal diseases.

DAISY. I know, I already have. It's just that during the sex, there's always 10 or 20 seconds during which I forget *who I am* and *where I am*. And that's why I'm so obsessive. But it's ridiculous to spend hours and hours seeking sex just really in order to find those 10 or 20 seconds. It's so *time-consuming!* I mean, no wonder I never get that paper on "Gulliver's Travels" done.

VOICE. Oh, you still haven't done that paper?

DAISY. No. I've been a freshman for five years now. I'm never going to graduate. At registration every fall, people just laugh at me.

VOICE. That's the end of our 53rd session. See you Tuesday. (*Lights change.*)

DAISY. (*Incensed.*) I mean it's the *inconsistency* I hate them most for! One minute they're cooing and cuddling and feeding me Nyquil, and the next minute they're turning on the gas jets, or lying on the floor, or threatening to step on my back. How *dare* they treat me like that? What's the matter with them! I didn't ask to be brought into the world. If they didn't know how to raise a child, they should have gotten a dog; or a kitten—they're more independent—or a *gerbil!* But left me *unborn.*

VOICE. That's the end of our 215th session. (*Lights change.*)

DAISY. I passed this couple on the street yesterday, and they had this four year old walking between them, and the two parents were fighting and you could just *tell* that they were insane. And I wanted to snatch that child from them and . . .

VOICE. And what?

DAISY. I don't know. Hurl it in front of a car, I guess. It was too late to save it. But at least it would be dead.

VOICE. That's the end of our 377th session. (*Lights change.*)

DAISY. (*Worn out by years of talking.*) Look, I suppose my parents aren't actually evil, and maybe my plan of hiring a hit person to kill them is going too far. They're not evil, they're just disturbed. And they mean well. *But meaning well is not enough.*

VOICE. How's your "Gulliver's Travels" paper going?

DAISY. I'm too depressed.

VOICE. I'm afraid I'm going to be on vacation next week.

DAISY. (*Unwilling to discuss this.*) I'm not happy with my present name.

VOICE. I'll just be gone a week.

DAISY. I wore a dress last week.

VOICE. I won't be gone that long.

DAISY. And I slept with thirty people.

VOICE. I hope you enjoyed it.

DAISY. And I can't be responsible for what I might do next week.

VOICE. Please, *please,* I need a vacation.

DAISY. All right, all right, take your stupid vacation. I just hope it rains.

VOICE. You're trying to manipulate me.

DAISY. Yes, but I mean well. (*Lights change. Very dark, a very pessimistic anger.*) Doctor. I've been in therapy with you for *ten* years now. I have been a college freshman for six years, and a college sophomore for four years. The National Defense loan I have taken to pay for this idiotic education will take me a *lifetime* to repay. (*His voice sounds lost.*) I don't know. I just feel sort of, well, stuck.

VOICE. Yes?

DAISY. Oh. And I had another memory I'd forgotten, something else my parents did to me. It was during that period I stayed in the laundry pile.

VOICE. (*His voice betraying a tiny touch of having had enough.*) Yes?

DAISY. My mother had promised me I could have ice cream if I would just stand up for ten minutes and not lie in the laundry, and then when I did stand up for ten minutes, it turned out she had forgotten she was defrosting the refrigerator and the ice cream was all melted. (*Sighs.*) I mean, it was so typical of her. (*Suddenly starts to get heated up.*) She had a college education. *Who could forget they were defrosting the refrigerator???* I mean, don't you just hate her?

VOICE. How old are you?

DAISY. Twenty-seven.

VOICE. Don't you think it's about time you let go of all this?

DAISY. What?

VOICE. Don't you think you should move on with your life?

40

Yes, your parents were impossible, but that's already happened. It's time to move on. Why don't you do your damn "Gulliver's Travels" paper? Why don't you decide on a name? My secretary has writer's cramp from changing your records from Rocky to Butch to Cain to Abel to Tootsie to Raincloud to Elizabeth the First to Elizabeth the Second to PONCHITTA PEARCE TO MARY BAKER EDDY! I mean, we know you had a rough start, but PULL YOURSELF TOGETHER! You're smart, you have resources, you can't blame them forever. MOVE ON WITH IT! (*Daisy has listened to the above embarrassed and uncomfortable, not certain how to respond. Then:*)
DAISY. FUCK YOU! (*Blackout.*)

SCENE 5

The home of John and Helen. A big box with a bow on it; on top of it a smaller box with a bow on it. A large banner that says, "Happy Birthday, Ponchitta." John has two bottles of vodka, Helen is using a Vicks inhaler.

HELEN. (*Inhaling.*) Mmmmmmm, I love this aroma. It almost makes me wish I had a cold. (*Inhales.*) Mmmmmm, delicious. Oh, there are pleasurable things in life. (*Calls off-stage.*) Daisy, dear, are you almost ready? We want to see how you look in your present.
JOHN. I thought his name was Ponchitta. (*Pronounced: Poncheat-a.*)
HELEN. John, we've been telling you all day, he called himself Ponchitta only for the month of March several years ago. He's been calling himself Charles Kuralt for the last several years, and now that he's turned thirty, as a gift to me, he's decided to go back to the name of Daisy. (*Calls.*) Daisy! We're waiting for you.
JOHN. I wish someone would've told me. I would've changed the banner.
HELEN. The banner's a lovely gesture, John. We all appreciate it. No one gives a fuck what's on it. I'm sorry, I don't mean to swear. No one gives a shit what's on it. Daisy, dear! Mommy and Daddy want to see you in your present. (*Enter Daisy, wearing*

41

a Scottish kilt; he looks somewhat pained, but has decided to be polite and not make waves. He holds his pants.)

HELEN. (*Admiring the kilt.*) Ohhhhh. Do you like it, dear?

DAISY. I'm not certain.

HELEN. Now it's not a dress, I want to make that very clear. It's a Scottish *kilt*. Scottish *men* wear them in the highlands, and all that air is wonderful for your potency if you're wearing boxer shorts rather than those awful jockey shorts that destroy your semen. Isn't that so, John?

JOHN. I wasn't listening.

HELEN. (*Making the best of things.*) That's right, you weren't listening. None of us were. All our heads were elsewhere. (*To Daisy.*) Your father's become a Christian scientist, and we're all so pleased. Now when he cuts himself, we don't even put a bandaid on him, we just watch him bleed.

JOHN. (*Cheerful, telling a fun anecdote.*) Cut myself this morning. Shaving. A nasty slice on the bottom of my foot. Between the vodka and the dalmane and then the weight of the razor, I fell right over. (*Laughs.*) Then trying to get up, I sliced my foot. Mother wouldn't let me put a bandaid on because she thinks I've become a Christian scientist.

HELEN. (*Firmly.*) That's right. That's what I do think. Ponchitta, dear, I'm sorry, I mean Daisy, you're so silent. Do you like your birthday present?

DAISY. Did you give this to me because you thought I'd like it because you're insane, or did you give it to me as a sort of nasty barb to remind me that you dressed me as a girl the first fifteen years of my life?

HELEN. (*Sincerely.*) I gave it to you because I thought you'd like it. Because I'm insane. I'm insane because I stayed in a bad marriage and didn't do what I was supposed to do with my life. But I'm not bitter. And now that your father's become a Christian scientist, I'm going to become a Jehovah's Witness and go to the supermarket *forcing* people to take copies of "The Watchtower." Perhaps "The Watchtower" will publish me. Certainly somebody has to, someday.

JOHN. Your mother's going through a religious phase. Cocktail, anyone? (*Offers one of the bottles.*)

HELEN. Your father calls drinking from a bottle a cocktail. It's

42

sort of adorable really. No, dear, but you have one. Oh, I'm enjoying life so much today. And you've turned thirty, and that means I'm getting nearer to death and have wasted my youth — oh, it cheers me up. Happy birthday, dear. (*Kisses Daisy.*)

JOHN. He hasn't opened up his other presents.

HELEN. Yes, Daisy dear, we have other presents. Here's one. (*Daisy puts his pants down on the couch and opens small box. It's a can, which when opened a large "snake" pops out of, just as happened to baby in first scene. Daisy is startled. Helen and John laugh in delight.*) Daisy always loved surprises. And now open the bigger box. (*Daisy opens bigger box — Nanny comes springing out of the box, shrieking, much like the snake did. Daisy falls over backward.*)

NANNY. AAAAAAAAAAAAAAGGGGGGGHHHHH!!! Whoogie! Whoogie! Whoogie! Surprise!!!!!

HELEN. Everybody sing!

HELEN, JOHN & NANNY. (*Sing, to the tune of "Frere Jacques."*)
Happy birthday, happy birthday,
Daisy dear, Daisy dear,
Happy, happy birthday,
Happy, happy birthday,
Happy birthday, happy birthday.

DAISY. *Who is this???*

NANNY. I'm your Auntie Mame! (*Laughs.*) No, just kidding. I'm the ANTI-CHRIST! (*Laughs.*) No, just kidding. (*Fondly.*) I'm your Auntie Nanny. (*Helen brings Daisy over to Nanny, who remains in the box.*)

HELEN. This is Nanny. Don't you remember Nanny?

DAISY. I remember something. God knows what. Why did you sing "Happy Birthday" to the wrong melody?

HELEN. Well, Nanny told us you have to pay a royalty to sing the real "Happy Birthday" melody. The selfish people who wrote the stupid melody don't have to lift a finger for the rest of their fucking lives, while I have to sweat and slave over the Cliff Notes to "The Thorn Birds." (*Pause.*) And all because your father has never been able to earn a living. (*Looks at John; says with total, grim sincerity:*) Oh why don't you just keel over and die? (*Laughs.*) Ha, ha, just kidding, I'm fine.

NANNY. (*To Daisy, in babytalk voice.*) Helllloooo. Helllloooo. What pwetty bwue eyes oo have. Cooooo. Cooooo. (*Suddenly.*)

SHUT UP! Comin' back to you, honey?

DAISY. Slightly. I try not to remember too much. It doesn't get me anywhere.

JOHN. (*Sings drunkenly, to the correct melody.*) Happy birthday to you, ha- . . .

HELEN. SHUSH! There are spies from ASCAP everywhere. (*John turns his head with some trepidation, looking for the spies.*)

NANNY. It's so nice to see one of my babies grown up. And what a pretty dress. The plaid matches your eyes.

HELEN. It's not a dress, Nanny. It's a *kilt.*

NANNY. Well, whatever it is, it's very becoming.

JOHN. (*Sings.*) Happy birthday . . .

HELEN. Please, John, *please.* (*Starts to get tears in her voice.*) We can't afford to pay the royalty. (*Starts to cry.*)

NANNY. (*To Helen, soothingly.*) There, there. SHUT UP! Ha, ha. (*Helen looks startled; then she and Nanny laugh and embrace.*) Oh, all my babies grow up so strong and healthy, I'm so pleased. What does baby do for a living?

HELEN. He goes to college. He was a freshman for six years, and he's been in sophomore slump for seven years.

NANNY. Thirteen years of college. Baby must be very smart.

HELEN. He's been having trouble writing his Freshman expository writing paper on "Gulliver's Travels." How's that going, Rocky, I'm sorry, I mean Daisy?

DAISY. I finished it. I thought I'd read it to you.

HELEN. Oh, this will be a treat. John, are you still there? John? Daisy is going to read to us.

NANNY. Let me just put on my glasses. (*Puts on her glasses, listens attentively.*)

DAISY. (*Reads from a sheet of paper.*) "'Gulliver's Travels' is a biting, bitter work that . . . depresses me greatly."

HELEN. Oh, I like it so far.

DAISY. "By the end of the book, Gulliver has come to agree with the King of Brobdingnag's assessment that mankind is the quote 'most pernicious race of little odious vermin that nature ever suffered to crawl upon the surface of the earth,' unquote. At the end of the book, Gulliver rejects mankind and decides he prefers the company of horses to humans. We are meant to find Gulliver's disgust with humanity understandable, but also to see that he has by now gone mad. However, I find that I do not wish to write papers analyzing these things anymore as I agree with Gulliver and find most of the world, including teachers, to be less worthwhile to speak to than horses. However, I don't like horses either, so I have decided after thirteen years of schooling that I am not meant to go to college and so I am withdrawing. Fuck your degree, I am going to become a bus driver."

HELEN. Oh I think that's excellent, I think you'll get a very good grade. John, wasn't that good? And how interesting you're going to become a bus driver. You've always been drawn to buses.

NANNY. I love buses too! I adore *all* public transportation. The danger of derailing, the closeness of the people, the smells, the dirt. I'm sort of like a bacteria!—wherever I am, I thrive. (*Smiles at Daisy.*)

DAISY. I'm glad you like the paper. I should also tell you that I'm getting married.

HELEN. (*Taken aback.*) Married? How fascinating. John, I feel you're not participating in this conversation.

JOHN. How do you spell dipsomaniac, I wonder?

HELEN. John, you're too young to write your memoirs. Besides, I'm the writer in the family.

DAISY. I wasn't really intending to get married, but she's pregnant.

HELEN. (*More taken aback.*) Pregnant, how lovely.

JOHN. D-I-P . . .

HELEN. John, participate in your life now. This isn't a spelling bee, this is a parent-child discussion.

DAISY. She's the 1,756th person I've slept with, although only the 877th woman.

HELEN. (*Slight pause.*) This conversation is just so interesting I don't know what to do with it.

DAISY. I don't think I love her, but then I don't use that word; and I do think I like her. And her getting pregnant just seemed sort of a sign that we should go ahead and get married. That, and the fact that I had taken her phone number.

JOHN. S-O-M . . .

NANNY. (*Sings.*) K-E-Y, M-O-U-S-E.

JOHN. Yes, thank you.

NANNY. Well, I think it's marvelous. Congratulations, Daisy.

HELEN. Well, your father and I will have lots of advice to give you. Don't give the baby Nyquil until it's about three. We made a mistake with you.

DAISY. I don't really wish to hear your advice.

HELEN. Well, we listened to your awful paper. You can at least do us the courtesy of listening to whatever garbage we have to say.

JOHN. (*Looks out.*) Oh, dear, here comes that owl again. (*Ducks, bats at air.*)

HELEN. Oh, your father's having problems again. John, dear, try to spell delirium tremens. That's a fun word.

JOHN. Z-B-X . . .

HELEN. No, dear, that's *way* off. Oh, God, he's going to be spelling all night long now. He's impossible to talk to when he's spelling. But, Daisy, you're here, and we'll talk, won't we? I've made you a delicious dinner. I've ordered up Chinese.

DAISY. I don't really think I can stay for dinner.

HELEN. But it's your birthday. I don't like Chinese food. What should I do with it?

DAISY. I hesitate to say.

HELEN. Pardon?

DAISY. I feel I must tell you that I've decided I don't think I should speak to you or father for a few years and see if I become less angry.

HELEN. Angry? Why are you angry?

DAISY. Let me see if I can answer that. (*Thinks.*) No, I don't think I can. Sorry. So, thank you for the kilt, and I better be going.

HELEN. Going?

NANNY. Baby, dear, let me give you some advice before you go. Get a *lot* of medical check-ups. Aside from your promiscuity, your parents exposed you to lead, asbestos, and red dye #2 from this little toy you had. Also, avoid acid rain, dioxin contamination, and any capsule tablets that might have cyanide in them. Try to avoid radiation and third degree burns after the atomic explosions come. And, finally, work on having a sense of humor. Medically, humor and laughter have been shown to physically help people to cope with the tensions of modern life that can be otherwise internalized, leading to cancer, high blood pressure, and spastic colon. (*Smiles.*) Well! It was very nice to

46

see you, best of luck in the future; and Helen, if you'd just mail me back to Eureeka, California, at your earliest convenience, I'd much appreciate it. (*Nanny disappears back into her box.*)

DAISY. What toy was she talking about?

HELEN. Oh who knows? Nanny's memory is probably starting to go. She must be about 103 or so by now. Resilient woman.

JOHN. D-E-L . . .

HELEN. Oh, delirium. Better start, darling.

JOHN. E-R-I . . .

DAISY. Well, I must be going now.

HELEN. Oh. Oh, stay a little longer, Daisy dear.

DAISY. (*Trying to be kind.*) Very well. (*Sits for about a count of three.*) Well, that's about it. (*Stands again.*) I think I'll just give you this kilt back, and I'll call you in a few years if I feel less hostile.

HELEN. That would be lovely, thank you, Daisy. (*He gives her back the kilt. He picks up his trousers from the couch, but does not take the time to put them on, he just heads for the door. At the door he stops and looks at his mother. She looks hurt and bewildered. He looks at her with regret, and some awful combination of dislike and tenderness.*)

DAISY. (*Softly.*) Goodbye. (*Daisy leaves.*)

HELEN. (*Recites, a great sense of loss in her voice.*)
"How sharper than a serpent's tooth
It is to have an ungrateful child."
John, what's that from?

JOHN. D-E-L . . .

HELEN. What's that *from,* John?

JOHN. E-R-I, M-O-U-S-E. There! But what's delirimouse?

HELEN. God only knows, John. (*John sees the kilt Helen is holding.*)

JOHN. Oh, another kilt.

HELEN. No, dear. Daisy gave it back. He said some very rude things, and then he left.

JOHN. Oh. Maybe he was angry about the banner.

HELEN. (*Sarcastically.*) Yes. Maybe that's it. Nonetheless, "to err is human, to forgive, divine." What's that from?

JOHN. "Bartlett's Famous Quotations."

HELEN. Oh, you're just *useless.* Nanny, what's that from? Also, "how sharper than a serpent's tongue" — "tooth!" — what's that from?

NANNY. (*From within box; irritated.*) I have nothing more to

47

say. Send me to the post office.

HELEN. Send me to the post office. What an orderly life Nanny leads. How I envy that.

JOHN. Uh oh. (*Ducks another owl.*)

HELEN. They're low-flying little beasts, aren't they, John? John, I wonder if I'm too old to have another baby? We could try again. (*John ducks again.*) But perhaps you're not in the mood tonight. Well, we can talk about it tomorrow. (*Looks sadly out, feels alone.*) "Tomorrow and tomorrow and tomorrow." (*Very sad.*) John, what's that from? Nanny? (*No response from either; she sighs.*) One loses one's classics. (*Stares out. Lights dim.*)

SCENE 6

The bassinet from the first scene of the play in a spot. Daisy, dressed normally in men's clothing, enters with a young woman named Susan. Susan is pretty and soft and sympathetic. They stand over the bassinet.

SUSAN. Hello, baby, hello. Coooo. Coooo. It's such a cute baby. Isn't it amazing how immediately one loves them?

DAISY. Yes, I guess so.

SUSAN. Say hello to the baby, Alexander.

DAISY. (*Somewhat stiffly.*) Hello.

SUSAN. Alexander, you're so stiff. Be more friendly to the child.

DAISY. Hello. (*He's better at it.*) Now we do know its sex, right?

SUSAN. Yes, it's a boy. Remember we sent out that card that said Alexander and Susan Nevsky are proud to announce the birth of their son, Alexander Nevsky, Jr.?

DAISY. Yes. *I* remember. I was just testing to check that you weren't insane and suddenly saying it was a girl.

SUSAN. No, I'm not insane. Hello, Alexander, Jr. (*To Daisy.*) How odd that you're called Alexander Nevsky. Do you have Russian ancestors?

DAISY. No, truthfully. I took the name myself. I liked the musical score to the movie. I've always had trouble with names.

SUSAN. Well, it's a very nice name. (*Baby starts to cry.*)

48

DAISY. Oh, my God, it's crying.

SUSAN. Oh dear. What should we do, I wonder?

DAISY. I'm not certain. (*They pause for a while.*) Probably we should hold it. (*Susan picks the baby up.*)

SUSAN. Instinctively that feels right. There, there. It's all right. It's all right. (*Baby stops crying.*)

DAISY. Goodness, how did you do that?

SUSAN. Here, you try. (*Hands him the baby. Daisy holds the baby rather awkwardly; the baby starts to cry.*)

DAISY. He doesn't like me.

SUSAN. Well, bounce him a little. (*Daisy does.*)

DAISY. There, there. (*Baby stops crying.*)

SUSAN. Sing to him, why don't you?

DAISY. (*Sings.*)

Hush, little baby, don't you cry,

Mama's gonna give you a big black. . . .

(*Daisy thinks, stares out quietly for a moment, changes the word.*)

. . . . poodle.

SUSAN. Are those the lyrics?

DAISY. I don't know the lyrics. (*Sings.*)

And if that big black poodle should attack,

Mama's gonna step on your little . . .

(*Catches himself again, redoes the whole line, making up the lyric as he goes:*)

Mama's . . . gonna . . . teach you . . . to bite it back,

And when baby grows up, big and strong,

Baby . . . can help mama . . . rewrite this song.

SUSAN. That's very sweet, Alexander. (*Daisy looks at Susan, smiles a little. They both sing to the baby.*)

BOTH.

Hush, little baby, don't you cry,

Mama's gonna give you a big black poodle,

And if that big black poodle should attack,

Mama's gonna teach you to bite it back,

And when baby grows up, big and strong,

Baby can help mama rewrite this song . . .

(*They keep humming to the baby as the lights dim to black.*)

PROP LIST

ACT I

SCENE 1

Bassinet — on casters

Couch — built so bed pushes through

Bookshelf w/ books & 2 toy ducks as bookends; one w/ vodka bottle inside — On wall

Umbrella stand w/ umbrellas — Next to door

Window w/ Venetian blinds — On wall

Carpetbag — contains jar with pop-out snake (jar looks like a gift) — Nanny

Baby — wrapped in pink blanket — In bassinet

2 one dollar bills — Nanny (inside lapel)

SCENE 2

Blanket; three pillows — On bed

Helen's novel — novel is stack of loose sheets of paper; written in longhand — Helen (L.)

Nyquil bottle — with plastic cup on top with drinkable liquid — Nanny (L.)

SCENE 3

Chopped meat — in small carton — John (L.)

Red toy — makes funny noise — Cynthia (from pocket)

Mommie Dearest — hardbound — Cynthia (from shelf)

ACT II

SCENE 1

Park bench

Can; beat up looking: used as ashtray — On ground next to bench

Tree

Cigarette & lighter — Helen

Knitting needles & yarn in bag — Kate

Family Circle magazine — Angela

Pills in small pill box — Angela

Canvas tote bag — Angela

SCENE 2

Many toys around room — Teddy bears; plastic rings; educational toys; including small plastic doll (head and arms come off easily) — On floor

Pile of laundry — w/ legs of child sticking out one end; pile is weighted to weight of small child (30-40 lbs.); sheet wrapped around pile so can tie it and lift bundle

2 toy ducks, one with vodka bottle inside — On shelf

SCENE 3

Desk; 2 chairs

Standing American flag

Calendar; clock — On wall

Intercom — On desk

Black candle — In drawer of desk

Daisy's essay; in vinyl binder — Miss Pringle

SCENE 5

Large box with bow — w/ place inside for Nanny to sit; lid comes off; box should look wrapped

Small box with bow — contains snake in jar; wrapped to match large box

Large banner — w/ large letters glued on to say "Happy Birthday Ponchitta"; w/ pins so can be hung on wall

2 gin bottles — John (on couch)

Vicks inhaler — Helen

"Gulliver's Travels" essay — Daisy (in pocket)

SCENE 6

Baby with blue blanket — In bassinet

COSTUME PLOT

ACT I

SCENE 1

HELEN — Dress; pumps; pearl necklace.

JOHN — Jacket; sweater vest; shirt; tie; corduroy pants; tan bucks (Bill's).

NANNY — Navy blue suit; hat; shoes; white gloves.

CYNTHIA — Denim jumper; tie-dyed tee-shirt; cotton Chinese shoes; hospital bracelet; fall; headscarf; pregnant pillow.

SCENE 2

HELEN — *Flannel nightgown.*

JOHN — *Flannel pajamas.*

NANNY — *Flannel nightgown; slippers; hairnet w/ rollers.*

HELEN — *Trenchcoat; rain hat; pumps (same as above) (nightgown underneath).*

HELEN — Remove trenchcoat; rain hat; pumps.

CYNTHIA — Same as above; not pregnant.

ACT II

SCENE 1

HELEN — Pullover; pants; pumps (same as above); Trenchcoat (same as above).

ANGELA — Jogging suit; headband; running shoes; glasses.

KATE — Jeans; turtleneck; headscarf; sneakers.

SCENE 2

HELEN — Same as II-1 — no trenchcoat.

JOHN — Shirt (buttoned collar); pants; blue terrycloth bathrobe; slippers.

SCENE 3

PRINCIPAL — Dress; shoes; gold chains.

MISS PRINGLE — Skirt & blouse; sweater; shoes; hair clips.

Denotes quick-change

SCENE 4

DAISY — Shirtwaist dress; Running shoes; athletic socks; underdressed in shirt; cords.

DAISY — Remove dress, toss off stage left.

SCENE 5

HELEN — Party dress; dyed-to-match shoes; party hat.

JOHN — White shirt; cardigan sweater; trousers; tie shoes; tie & tie clip; party hat.

DAISY — *Kilt; oxfords; socks & shirt from II-4; pants (carry over arm).*

NANNY — Same as in Act I; glasses (in box).

SCENE 6

DAISY — *Blazer; tie; pants (ones carried in II-5); shoes.*

SUSAN — Dress; shoes; hair ribbon; necklace.

ACT II

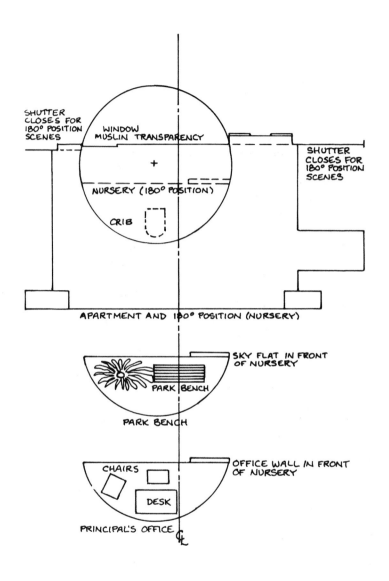

SHUTTER
CLOSES FOR
180° POSITION
SCENES

WINDOW
MUSLIN TRANSPARENCY

SHUTTER
CLOSES FOR
180° POSITION
SCENES

NURSERY (180° POSITION)

CRIB

APARTMENT AND 180° POSITION (NURSERY)

SKY FLAT IN FRONT
OF NURSERY

PARK BENCH

PARK BENCH

OFFICE WALL IN FRONT
OF NURSERY

CHAIRS

DESK

PRINCIPAL'S OFFICE

SCENE DESIGN
" BABY WITH THE BATHWATER"
DESIGNED BY LOREN SHERMAN

AUTHOR'S NOTES

I have gotten into the habit of writing author's notes to the acting editions of my plays. I have mostly received good feedback on doing this from people, though recently a director about to do a play of mine told me he found the notes "annoying." So I wanted to stress that these notes are not meant to declare by fiat how my plays *must* be done, but just as guidelines to indicate the kind of acting and directing tone I had in mind when I wrote the play. To quote another writer on the issue, here's Tom Stoppard quoted in the New York Times (Nov. 22, 1983) during rehearsals for "The Real Thing":

> "For Mr. Stoppard, whose earlier plays include "Travesties" and "Rosencrantz and Guildenstern are Dead," such daily involvement [of attending rehearsal] is customary practice with a new production. 'You save people quite a lot of time,' he notes. 'You can answer things it would take time to work out, and maybe without me it would be worked out with the wrong answer. It's not a question of how it *has* to be, but you do want people to know what you meant. They can make a different choice, but it's important that they know what they're changing.'"

I can't be at rehearsals for every production of a play of mine, so these notes are my attempt to communicate what I had in mind and to offer, I hope, shortcuts on some problems. You always have to add common sense and the particular strong points and weak points of your cast, and go from there. But every script has some moments that are ambiguous or confusing alone on the page; and I also think the playing tone of my plays is not always the easiest thing to figure out. That's the reason I offer these notes. And so enough of this defensive introduction. (The director who complained about the notes, by the way, ended up directing a very successful production.)

"Baby with the Bathwater" has been produced twice as of these notes: its premiere at the American Repertory Theatre in Cambridge, Massachusetts in the spring of 1983, and its New York premiere at Playwrights Horizons in the fall of 1983. I saw and enjoyed the Cambridge production, but I was more involved in the New York production that followed, and so most of these notes will refer to things I learned from that production.

Jerry Zaks, who directed "Baby with the Bathwater" in New York and who has previously directed "Sister Mary Ignatius Explains It All For You" and the off-Broadway version of "Beyond Therapy," has a very good sense of how to keep genuine human feelings in my plays so they don't shoot out into the stratosphere as only surreal farces, but he also knows how to balance the "human" qualities with a good comedy director's sense of pace and appropriate exaggeration. (As the Bible, or perhaps George Abbott, says, there is a time for exaggeration, and there is a time for saying the line sincerely.)

One thing Jerry worked for from the start was that Helen and John want to be good parents, that they do, as Daisy says later in a psychiatric session, "mean well." That's probably easier to figure out about John, who is clearly less tempestuous than Helen and who does often say things that make sense and show concern for the baby. But it's important to find these sympathetic motives in Helen as well. The opening moments of the play (up through Helen's "Don't call the child a baked potato") should be filled with genuine and happy love for the child and for each other. (This love should be genuine, though it can certainly be immature: W.H. Macy and Christine Estabrook both got appropriate audience laughter when they giggled with pleasure after he compliments her hair and she says "Thank you." It felt a little bit like children playing house — sweet, but immature, uninformed.)

On the other hand, it's important that Helen's ferocity not be ducked. She "means well," but when she screams "JOHN, LIVE UP TO YOUR RESPONSIBILITIES!" or (at the end of Act I) screams "I TOLD YOU NOT TO CALL IT A BAKED POTATO!", the actress must be willing to let John have it to the fullest extent of her vocal chords. She must not worry about "being sympathetic" to the audience. Although she is not meant to be "only" a monster, on some level and at some times she really *is* a monster — an emotional bully to John, and deeply frightened. The actress must commit to her large moments fully — both so her character is fulfilled and so that the comedy will work. The Act II in-the-park scene is written for Helen to be truly awful to Daisy, and the more vicious she is in the screaming (within the bounds of a kind of comic reality; one could turn it into a kind of psychodrama which would then not be funny and not have the tone I intended; we're back to common sense and instinct again) the funnier the scene should be, and the more serious the scene's implications for Helen and Daisy.

This is one of my less "realistic" plays, and the characters change mood and attitude more abruptly than they do in, say, "Sister Mary Ignatius." So two things on this. The first is to commit to whatever the character is saying fully. For instance, when Helen in the first scene has her "DNA" explanation speech of what the doctor said to her about how they can decide the child's sex "later," the actress should play only that she is presenting the facts as she was told them, as straight-forwardly and simply as possible. The speech is funny/effective when it sounds plausible because Helen finds it plausible; the actress should not in some way "cue" the audience that she knows the logic is cuckoo and that she is saying something funny.

The second bit of advice is somewhat connected, and has to do with the emotional switches. One moment Helen is telling Nanny not to push her around, and the next moment Helen melts into little-girlishness (on being promised an ice cream soda) and says "I love you, Nanny." Just play those different emotions and attitudes fully and don't worry about how the transitions between them occur; trust that I've done that in the work itself.

Helen and John, though exaggerated, are fairly recognizable from life. The characters of Nanny and the Principal are a bit more surreal and Alice in Wonderland-like. Nanny is conceived as a kind of cracked Mary Poppins figure. She is also inconsistency incarnate, able to soothe the child with pleasant, soothing noises ("Wheeeeee; whaaaaaaa" etc.) and then suddenly get cross and scream "Shut up!" She also does fairly inexplicable things like (in the birthday scene near the end of the play) put on her glasses in order, apparently, to "hear" Daisy's essay better. There's no logic to this; it should be just committed to. (I read an interview with Dana Ivey, who originated Nanny in New York, in which she commented on acting in "Baby": "The Durang [play] is so filled with non sequiturs that you have to do each thing with total conviction — if you try to look for a stream of consciousness like you would for any other playwright, it

57

would just get in the way." So, to sum up, when in doubt, commit fully to whatever choice the script indicates and don't worry about the connectives if they don't seem apparent.)

When you cast Cynthia, be careful that you cast a sympathetic actress. Cynthia's story of her baby being eaten by the German shepherd is so awful that it's important that the actress' vibes be innately sweet so that it can become clear that Cynthia actually *does* love babies, it's just that she isn't very smart. The whole point of her character then becomes that her loving babies is not enough to "save" the two babies she comes in contact with. When she says to Nanny as she leaves, "I know what I'm doing," she absolutely doesn't, of course. But she's not an evil woman; she just really doesn't (as she says) "know any better."

It's also important to cast Cynthia with a sympathetic actress, because the roles of Angela, Miss Pringle, and especially Susan should also be very sympathetic. I'd like to add a stage direction regarding Susan and the last scene that I took out of the text itself because it hurt the flow of reading but which remains essential to the final scene's meaning:

> SUSAN is pretty and soft and sympathetic. The sense of her and DAISY at the end of the play is that though obviously there will be problems, they may indeed be better parents than the previous people in the play. SUSAN is played by the same actress who plays CYNTHIA; however, be certain that she looks substantially different than she did when she was CYNTHIA, and that this be her prettiest and most normal appearance.

Here are some miscellaneous thoughts on various issues and moments in the play.

Blond hair for John. It seems in casting the play it is preferable that John have blond hair, better for his "vibes." However, if the best person for the part doesn't have blond hair, please change Helen's lines in scene 1 to reflect this. Change it (p. 6), I think, to "You have curly hair. I don't like men with curly hair. I like men with straight hair, but I'm afraid of them. I'm not afraid of you. I hate you." (If your actor has straight, non-blond hair, then make the lines go "You have straight hair. I don't like men with straight hair." etc.)

Strength in John. John is obviously not quite Helen's match;

however, let him be successfully asserting himself when the script gives him the opportunity (chiefly in his "Now enough of all this arguing!" speech on p. 15).

Cynthia's red toy that goes tingle-tangle. Make sure it's large enough to be visually recognizable to the audience at the end of the play when John and Helen offer it to baby.

Focus in the novel-reading sequence. When Cynthia is reading from (my version of) "Mommie Dearest," I found it helpful to let her reading catch John and Helen's attention when she speaks; when she finishes, they go back to their arguing. And while they have their argument lines, Cynthia can "mark" time from her reading by making friendly faces and noises to the baby.

In Act II, Scene 1, the character of Kate. Just a clarification since it hasn't been crystal clear to actresses approaching the part. Kate is sensible, logical, very opinionated. She is, in a way, a natural enemy to Helen; if they were on a women's committee together, they'd kill one another. So once Helen enters the scene, Kate finds herself disapproving of Helen quite a bit; she doesn't confront her too directly at first out of a normal politeness; later she is careful because she starts to realize how really "off" Helen is; she might be dangerous. Kate is a realist par excellence; that's why she has no trouble saying blunt things if they're true ("no one in our family is particularly good looking"), or in her most direct "confront" of Helen, "that's no way to bring up a child." When Helen leaves the scene, Kate becomes annoyed at Angela's do-nothing attitude; when she says "Alright, we won't do anything about her. We'll wait until we read about the child *dead* in the newspaper," there's a kind of irritation in her voice that implies if the child is found dead it will be all Angela's fault for not pursuing this issue, although she clearly isn't willing to pursue it on her own. And, finally, once Angela rattles on about what makes her depressed and then pops her "mood elevators," Kate realizes she has another, different kind of loony on her hand; her "Well, fine" as she edges away is meant to (comically) indicate that she thinks Angela is quite a nut.

Also in the park. Be sure to differentiate vocal levels and energy with the mothers calling out to their children, and talking to one another. Obviously Helen is quite ferocious with some of

59

her shouting, but the other two mothers should also be louder calling to their children than they are just talking to one another.

The toy duck prop. At American Rep. the prop person constructed a wooden duck (which looked somewhat like a wooden duck decoy) that had a hinged opening on its back, and the vodka bottle fit into this "cabinet" in the duck's back. At Playwrights Horizons, the prop man hollowed out a fluffy-looking yellow duck (that looked like it would go on a child's bed) and fit it like a glove over the vodka bottle; the cap of the bottle more or less came out the duck's ass. With this version, John drank from the bottle without taking it out of its "duck holder." Before John picked up the "duck bottle," however, it just looked like a regular child's stuffed duck. Both these solutions seem fine to me.

When Helen does her vocal "exercises" ("toy duck, toy duck; polly wolly windbag, polly wolly windbag," etc.), I can barely explain to the various actresses what I am intending except to say that it's the kind of nonsense talking someone might do when they're so tired and/or fed up that they just don't want to bother articulating thoughts or words anymore. There's a bit of a punishing quality meant too, since she is speaking aloud in a room that includes John but is not saying anything that he could possibly respond to. And, all that aside, the actress shouldn't "do" too much with them, just say them simply, rhythmically, and without too much emotion except a touch of "oh, if only one of us were dead." You know. You feel that way sometimes. Don't you?

The Principal scene. She has a line that goes "Yes. Uh huh. Uh huh. Yes, I see. Uh huh. Uh huh. Go on." I don't quite know how to articulate what I want to say (toy duck, toy duck, toy duck), but here goes. Each one of these phrases should be done in the exact same, unemphasized way that one would say "Yes, I see." One should not differentiate them, stress one more than the other. Their inflection is much the same as we all do on the phone listening to someone tell a long story (uh huh; uh huh; yes; hmmn), only the principal's words are odd because, of course, she's already listened to the story and is *now* giving her reaction. Dana Ivey did it this way instinctively first time out, but other people have been a bit thrown by it. Do you follow what I mean, toy duck toy duck?

I must pull myself together.

Tiny point. When Principal *does* put her hand over her mouth to listen, finally, to what Miss Pringle has to say, I find it important that she actually *does* put her hand over her mouth; she's been so talkative that otherwise I get distracted thinking she's going to speak up again. Once Miss Pringle gets past the title and into the first sentence of the essay, however, I think the Principal should shift to a more "normal" listening posture, her-hands-supporting-her-chin kind of thing. The only reason to go on about this moment is that it is very important that the actress playing the Principal cue the audience that they must give all their attention, finally, to Miss Pringle and the essay; and the Principal is so much fun (I had a great time writing this scene) that we must let the audience know not to expect anything more from the Principal during the essay.

Final point about this scene. It is written to vocally and emotionally peak from "Yes, but I *am* in a position of power!" on through til the final line ("Who cares if she's dead as long as she publishes? Now get out of here!); you mustn't pull back at any point during these final lines, and the last line must be the biggest (or at least as big as "Yes, but I *am* in a position of power!").

The Daisy/Psychiatrist Section. In both productions the Voice has been done live by the same actor who plays John, and as long as your John doesn't have an overwhelmingly recognizable voice, I think that's the best idea. I've left the voice out of the program credits so as not to tip off the audience that we have a "psychiatrist" or a "voice" sequence; and as long as the actor is willing to forego that credit, that's preferable to me. If he definitely wanted the credit, please make it say "Voice" and not "Psychiatrist."

I think I've made this clear in the text itself now, but please please don't put blackouts in the "Daisy" scene; it hurts the flow and changes the feel from it being one long scene that has time jumps to being a long series of scenes with waits between them. (This is the one major disagreement I had with the American Rep. director.) Also, Daisy's change from dress to male clothes should not be done in the dark (unless it could *really* be done on the count of 1-2, which I doubt); it's much better to let the audience see him change, so the play *continues,* than to stop the action so we don't see the mechanics of the change. Let us see the mechanics; it's theatre, we'll accept it.

I've notated in Daisy's speech a lot of the coloring that I think should be there. For a lot of it, especially the long opening part of it, it should be kind of deadpan; among other things, Daisy doesn't know that his past has been that terrible really, and he's just recounting the facts. The only other thing I'll toss in is a phrase from Edith Oliver's praise (in *The New Yorker*) for Keith Reddin who played Daisy: "Keith Reddin . . . is the perfect Durang leading man, puzzled and gravely polite, until he finally asserts himself." Keith deserved the praise, but I quote it because Ms. Oliver's phrase itself — "puzzled and gravely polite" — is a terrific description of how I feel Daisy should be played for much of his speech, and for most of the Scene 5 birthday party.

The Scene 5 birthday party. Daisy is older (30), been in analysis, and for much of the scene is going along with his parents politely because to do otherwise would make a scene and not be worth it. John, batting owls, is clearly out to lunch. Helen is tricky. I've found actresses instinctively want to make all the lines "fake cheery" which is right for a lot of it, but not for all of it. Please excuse how many "acting adjectives" I've put in the playing text, but I can for instance understand the logic of Helen saying "Oh why don't you keel over and die" with a cheery insincerity, but I know (thanks to Christine Estabrook and to Dianne Wiest at a reading) that to do it sincerely and with utter hatred of your life is funnier and adds depth to the play and to the scene. Similarly, Helen is very, very sad and lost once Daisy leaves at the end of the scene; let her be that way; let it be the end of "Three Sisters" and "if only we knew." Weird farce with one foot in reality suddenly switching to sadness with *both* feet in reality — I've been discovering, I think, that this is the approach to take with most of my plays. Don't overdo the sad moments, but don't pass by them.

I think I've gone on already too long. Whatever your set, make the changes be as fast as possible. Long blackouts are comedy's enemy.

There is more than one way to do any play, so once again my apologies to actors for giving too many specifics; but to quote from Mr. Stoppard again, if you make another choice, "at least you will know what you're changing."

Christopher Durang
May, 1984